Thank God, I'm Free

The James Robison Story

JAMES ROBISON

Thank God, I'm Free

The James Robison Story

THOMAS NELSON PUBLISHERS
NASHVILLE

Published in Nashville, Tennessee, by Thomas Nelson, Inc., and distributed in Canada by Lawson Falle, Ltd., Cambridge, Ontario.

Printed in the United States of America.

Scripture quotations are from THE NEW KING JAMES VERSION of the Bible. Copyright © 1979, 1980, 1982, Thomas Nelson, Inc., Publishers.

Library of Congress Cataloging-in-Publication Data

Robison, James, 1943–
    Thank God, I'm free!

    1. Robison, James, 1943–   . 2. Evangelists—
United States—Biography. I. Title.
BV3785.R62A3 1987   269'.2'0924[B]   87–31439
ISBN 0-8407-7610-1

    3 4 5 6 — 92 91 90 89 88

With glory to God for all He continues to do in my life, I dedicate this book to those most precious to me: my wife, Betty; our children, Rhonda, Randy, and Robin.

Also to Rev. and Mrs. H. D. Hale who gave me a home and led me to Christ, and to the memory of my mother, Myra, and my father, Joe, whom I barely knew.

CONTENTS

The Want Ad Baby

I was raised as a child with two mothers and two fathers, which is not all that unusual in the 1980s but it was in the 1940s and 1950s when I was young. It was not the blessing some might suppose. Children who are raised that way today would probably agree.

The woman who cared for me during my first five years was Katie Bell Hale, the pretty sandy-haired wife of the Reverend Herbert Doyle Hale, the pastor of the Memorial Baptist Church in Pasadena, Texas. The Hales were Mommy and Daddy to me.

Then there was this other woman, who visited me every week or two. I didn't understand that she was my real mother. In fact, my memories of her before I was five are vague and disjointed. Once she took me to the circus. Most often, I went to stay with her for only a few days at a time.

She never lived in a home of her own. And she rarely lived in the same place long enough for me to visit it more than a few times. She always seemed to live at a half address, 1701 $1/2$ or

783 ½. Her room (or two at the most) was in the back or the basement or the attic of someone else's place. The only treat she ever seemed to have was peanut butter and jelly. She was nice to me and she obviously cared about me, but I always wanted to get back to my home and my parents: the Hales.

Then one day, when I was five, my "other mother" came to get me. Only something was different. My little cardboard suitcase was packed tight with everything I owned. She said, "You're going with me." It sounded so final, so absolute.

The Hales protested, saying something about this being too sudden and telling her how much they loved me. My other mother reminded them that they weren't really my parents and that she had the right to take me whenever she wanted to. When it was clear that I would be leaving, Mrs. Hale lay across her bed, wailing convulsively. Even Pastor Hale was weeping. I was petrified.

I raced to my bed and scrambled underneath, the only safe place I could think of. Pastor Hale gently pulled me out by one foot while I desperately tried to cling to the slick hardwood floor. Why were they making me go? It didn't appear that *any-one* was happy about what was happening.

My face contorted in pain, I walked down the front sidewalk with my heavy suitcase in one hand and my mother's hand in the other. I turned to see the tear-streaked faces of Mommy and Daddy Hale. I thought my life had come to an end.

In our simple clothes, dressed for the windless heat of the hottest August day of 1948, we trudged out to the highway. Mother had no money for bus or train fare. We hitchhiked all the way from Houston to Austin, 175 miles under a cloudless sky. We rode with families in cars, on the back of a cattle truck with the cows, and in the cab of a mail truck.

People were friendly, but I let no one, not even my mother, help me with my suitcase. I wouldn't part with it. I lifted it; I carried it; I held it; I sat on it. I wouldn't let anyone else touch it. My whole world was in that suitcase. I have it to this day, four decades later.

The worst part was that I didn't understand why everything had changed. Why wasn't I just visiting her like always, planning to go back to my home in Pasadena near Houston? Why didn't I have any choice? Why was it so sudden? One day I had a home and parents, and the next I was in the middle of nowhere, hitchhiking with a woman who had taken me away from those two wonderful people I loved. My tears were hidden in the sweat cascading down my face that day.

In the months and years ahead I would learn the reason, bit by bit, as my mother told me about herself and my real father. My real mother, Myra Wattinger, had been a drifter for years, a single parent of a son named Sidney. When a doctor told her first husband, John Wattinger, and her that she was infertile, they adopted Sidney. Not long after that, the marriage soured, and John Wattinger divorced her without giving her any alimony, even though he was a prominent contractor who eventually helped build the Texas State Capitol Building. Since her parents had died when she was an adolescent, my mother had to support herself and her son without any help.

In early 1943, my mother found a job taking care of an elderly man named Robison, who had several grown children living with him. (The name is pronounced just like Robinson, without the first *n*.)

Joe Robison, the oldest son, had been an alcoholic since his first drink at age nineteen. By now he was in his thirties, a tall, good-looking man with wavy hair. The rest of the family, particularly his sister Roberta, defended him and took care of him. Basically, he was on the rum and on the bum for the rest of his life.

Joe Robison found Myra Wattinger attractive and tried to seduce her. She put him off, finding him repulsive and assuming his advances were simply the results of drunken stupors. But the day came when only Joe and Myra were in the house, other than the elderly, sleeping Mr. Robison. Although the act was not violent and Myra was not physically injured, Joe Robison forced her. She was disgusted and humiliated, but more so when she discovered that she was pregnant. She was in disbelief—in her forties, divorced, barely scratching out a living, the victim of rape, and pregnant!

Joe Robison offered to marry her, but she would have nothing to do with him. She was desperate, unable to fathom how she could possibly raise an infant. More than one doctor had told her she should be unable to get pregnant; now others were telling her she might die in childbirth. Myra Wattinger sought an abortion, but in 1943, that was hard to come by. Her doctor said he simply wouldn't do it, and he wouldn't recommend it.

Nearly suicidal, she trudged to the home where she was staying and sat out on the screened-in back porch. She cried out to God as she had many times: "Lord, I'm carrying this child, and I don't know what to do."

God spoke to her, clearly if not audibly: "Have this baby. It will bring joy to the world."

Her heart leaped. Convinced her baby was a girl, she promised God she would name her Joy, and she lived in peaceful anticipation of this gift from the Lord until October 9, 1943, when she was admitted to the charity ward of St. Joseph's Hospital in Houston. She worked so hard and long in a nearly impossible delivery that she passed out just after she heard one nurse tell another, "That pitiful little baby."

The baby with curly black hair may have been in pitiful straits, but he was healthy. And he was me. They say I screamed and wriggled like a normal newborn, but my mother lay deathly still. The doctor checked her pulse and her blood pressure, then pulled a sheet over her face. "She's gone." On his way out, he motioned to the nurses and pointed at my mother. "Morgue," he said. They secured a litter from the hall and began the difficult transfer of the body from the bed. During the maneuver, the sheet slid from Mother's face, and a nurse saw her contorted expression. She was struggling to breathe.

The nurses worked over her for several minutes, their uniforms soaked through with sweat. When she came to, she saw two red-faced, panting women in white. "What happened?"

"Lady, we were fighting for your life."

They summoned the doctor and told him, "This woman is alive."

Mother told the doctor, "My baby's name is Joy."

He shook his head. "You can call that baby whatever you want, but it's a boy."

She prayed and thought of the disciples closest to Jesus: Peter, James, and John. She wanted her son, the one God had told her would bring joy to the world, to be close to Jesus. "James," she said. "I'll name him James." The birth certificate read James Wattinger, but Mother told everyone the truth. My name was James Robison. And after the question: "Legitimate?" the "no" box was checked.

The seriousness of Mother's situation hit her soon enough. She was a drifter, getting work where she could find it. She had hardly enough money to buy food, and no prospects for anything better. As much as it caused her the deepest pain imaginable to admit it, she knew her new baby was more than she could handle. She was already raising one child alone. Not a young woman anymore, she knew she couldn't afford to have someone take care of me all day while she worked.

She decided it would be better to let someone else raise me, so the day after I was born, she scraped together a few dollars for a short ad in a Houston newspaper:

WANTED—Loving, Christian couple to raise newborn boy. References required. Call. . . .

The balding, middle-aged Pastor Hale and his wife, Katie Bell, answered her ad because they had always wanted a son. They had a teenage daughter, but they were unable to have more children. So they visited my mother and fell in love with her three-week-old baby, promised to love him, to raise him as a Christian, and to let her visit him anytime she wanted. They were not wealthy, but as the pastor of a Southern Baptist Church with a constantly growing membership, Daddy Hale earned a comfortable living. To Mother, they were an answer to prayer.

Two years later, the Hales asked if they could adopt me, and my mother agreed. They had the papers drawn up, and she came to sign them. But with the pen in her hand, she changed her mind. "I won't release him," she told them, and she asked that they never bring up the subject again.

About that time Joe Robison was back in her life, finally talking her into marrying him. Perhaps she thought she had a chance to get me back and raise me herself. But it didn't work out. He was still a drunk, wouldn't stay with her, couldn't keep a job, and wound up more of a burden than a help. She soon divorced him, but she remained resolute about not letting the Hales adopt me.

Being raised by the local preacher and his wife meant that I was in church every time the doors were open. Though I was basically happy in that loving home, I was somewhat troubled by having to frequently leave with my other mother. I was unsettled, confused. I wasn't sure where I belonged, but I knew where I preferred to stay, and that was with the Hales.

Maybe because of my unsettled state, I was a holy terror in and around the church. I got into all kinds of mischief, from

14

sneaking into the nursery to steal crackers and mess up the cribs to being a general nuisance. The Hales tried to discipline me, but I was a tough little bully. Lots of people in the church thought I was a really bad kid, fighting all the time.

For a boy who was almost named Joy, I wasn't very joyful or content. I didn't know that I had been the product of a rape, that only a doctor's counsel and God's speaking to my mother kept me from being aborted. I didn't know that I was born in a charity ward to an unwed woman, or that she had advertised to have someone else raise me. All I knew was that I was different. My mom and dad were older than other kids' parents, and my other mother (I seemed to think of her in that way even after I learned she was my real mother) was older, too.

Then when I was a preschooler, my mother's adopted son, Sidney, left home to go to college, intending to eventually join the air force. (He would go on to become a highly decorated major before his retirement.) I remember his visiting me a couple of times at the Hales' home and when I was with my mother for a few days.

After he left, my mother thought I was all she had left in the world, and she wanted me back. That's why she came to Pasadena to get me that day. My life would never be same after that.

15

Adrift

The pain of leaving Mommy and Daddy Hale stayed with me for years, but amazingly, I adapted to the new situation. It wasn't fun. It wasn't easy. Mother had a tough time making ends meet. But my heart went out to her. She did love me. She did care about me. It was soon evident that she was all I had, and I was all she had.

Mother took me to live with Aunt Berta, who was my real father's older sister, and her friend, Thelma Warren (Timbo, to me). They became very special people in my life, befriending me and caring about me. Even when we moved out of their place, we never moved so far away that I couldn't see them occasionally.

For the next several years we moved five or six times a year, whenever conditions changed or a job ended or a rent bill came due that Mother couldn't pay. I was left with friends or relatives for days at a time, never knowing when Mother would return. I was so sad and distraught when she would leave me that I wouldn't even play. I just found the nook or cranny that had been assigned to me for a bed, and I went there and cried myself to sleep. Fortunately, she never left me with anyone unkind, but it didn't matter. I was always so sad when she left, and I didn't know when or if I would see her again.

When we were together, Mother was a very dominating woman. She needed me. She loved me. After a while, I thought the sun rose and set on her. Old before her years, she was still a striking woman, and she was extremely articulate. She wore me out, teaching me to speak correctly. Even now, I'm amazed at how I can extemporaneously construct sentences that make sense, even in front of a crowd. I owe that to my mother.

I could sit and listen to her talk for hours. Often, I did. She was as forceful and as powerful a communicator as you will ever meet. I adored her; I worshiped her. Only later in my life was I able to detect any inconsistencies in her. And even then, she was usually able to convince me that I was wrong.

She was the only constant in my life. I detested the places we lived, the clothes we wore, the food we ate. She always insisted on our eating what she called balanced meals, but they usually consisted of peanut butter and jelly sandwiches—which I still loved—for lunch and chicken or ground beef for supper with an inexpensive garden green of some kind.

Wherever we lived—and I could hardly keep track of all the places—was not *home*. It was an existence. Our few sticks of furniture consisted of a chair or two, a table, and two rickety beds. Mother would insist that though we were poor, we were all right. To me, we were not all right. I was embarrassed to death to think of anyone I knew at school ever seeing where I lived. I never invited anyone home, never accepted rides home, never told anyone where I lived.

Mother had an answer for or an idea about everything. She spoke often of God and about the Bible, and she was tuned in to the spirit world. But as much as she talked about God, she never went to church, seldom read a Bible, or even sent me to Sunday school. I was an adult before I realized that her view of Scripture limited her accuracy in discerning what voices she was really hearing.

As a six- and seven-year-old, I didn't have a redemptive thing in my life. My thoughts and actions were impure. It was almost as if an outside force affected my mind and thoughts.

When I was seven, we lived for a few months on a little farm near some Mexican people. One day in a barn, I was talking ugly to a beautiful, nine-year-old Mexican girl who couldn't figure out why a kid she thought was nice would talk that way. She stood near the barn door, and I was up in the hayloft, looking down at her. The look on her face didn't stop me. I felt like a bad kid, and I was acting like a bad kid. But suddenly, a voice inside me said, *This isn't right.*

I knew it was God. I just knew it. He was speaking clearly through my conscience. *This isn't right.*

It gave me only the briefest pause. I didn't care. I literally didn't care if it *was* God. What had He ever done for me? Mommy and Daddy Hale had believed in Him and worshiped Him and worked for Him and taken me to church and Sunday school. But here I was, a poor, nasty kid.

The voice said, *This isn't right,* and I shrugged it off. With my whole body, I was saying, *I don't care. I don't care if it's right or wrong or who thinks or says so, even God.*

The next thing I knew, I was tumbling through the air, as if in slow motion. I hadn't been watching where I was walking, and I stepped through the opening to the hayloft. My body turned end over end in the air, and I landed squarely on my back across a cement trough.

I was stunned. I felt as if I should have been broken in two. I struggled to my feet and took one step toward the girl, now just a few feet away. Her eyes were wide with terror. "Are you all right?" she managed.

I tried to speak, but I couldn't make a sound. My heart crashed within my chest, banging against my ribs. I couldn't even nod. I staggered another step. And then as distinctly as I've ever felt anything in my life, I felt my heart stop. I froze. My heart was still. And I fainted.

I came to a few seconds later, my heart racing again. The girl had rushed to me and grabbed me, screaming. I was terrified. I sat up and shushed her. "My heart stopped." She was speechless. "Don't say anything. Don't tell anyone! Promise?"

She nodded.

I eventually told my mother that I had fallen in the barn and that my heart had stopped. But I didn't tell her what I had been up to when it happened, and I certainly didn't tell her that I had shrugged off a clear warning from God. I knew He was there and He was watching and He cared about what I did. Ultimately, I put that scare behind me and was pretty much the same kid I had always been. I was so determined to do what I wanted to do. I had been dealt a raw deal in life, and I figured somebody somewhere owed me something.

The only positives in my life, besides the fact that my mother taught me to speak correctly, were my interests in reading and in sports. I wasn't a great student, but I loved to read. And all my anxieties and hostilities seemed to be vented when I had a ball to kick or hit or throw or somewhere to run. No one could outrun me, not even the older kids. I was running to or from something they would never understand, something not even I understood. But when I was running fast, my entire being was into it.

I lived and died for competition. Give me a chance to prove I was better than someone at something, and I'd go for it. The teacher had a bookworm program going in fourth grade. You got a worm section for every book you read, so the student with the longest bookworm at the end of the term would win. That was all the incentive I needed. There was nothing I wanted more.

I started school before I was five, so I was always the youngest in the class. And we moved so often, I was always the new kid, the kid no one knew, the one with no friends, the one picked last for all the ball teams. Well, the James Robison bookworm was going to circle that room and blow away all the competition!

I didn't cheat. The teacher had it set up in such a way that you really could read whatever books you chose. She pointed me toward biographies and started me with John Paul Jones. I thought the book was pretty good, so I read about George Washington, Abraham Lincoln, Kit Carson, Buffalo Bill, Wyatt Earp, Wild Bill Hickok, Davy Crockett, Daniel Boone, the presidents, the generals, and the statesmen from the United States and Europe. If I didn't read about a leader, it was only because no one told me he was a leader.

Somehow, in the midst of all that reading, I developed some skills and even some admirable qualities. A lot of it had to have rubbed off. I didn't notice any immediate difference in my behavior, but I must have stored things away for future use. I became a voracious reader on a wide range of topics, and I still am. My vocabulary, my comprehension, and my coherence improved. By the way, I won that bookworm reading contest hands down.

When we moved briefly to East Austin, I was scared. The Latin American street gangs ruled the area, and I was still in elementary school. I was afraid to walk to school, and Aunt Berta knew it. I could always count on her for something special. She gave me a beautiful, brand-new bicycle with all the extras. The first day I rode it to school, I got there without any trouble, but I felt conspicuous. It was colorful, bright, and shiny. I was proud of it, but scared, too. The bike didn't go unnoticed.

That afternoon, I was two blocks from home when I was ambushed. Older boys on bikes came at me from all sides. I slid to a stop, just as they smashed into my bike, knocking me down, scraping my elbows. They rode over my bike until the handlebars were bent upside-down, the spokes were smashed, and the reflectors were broken. They screamed at me, calling me chicken, and laughed as I stood there crying while they stripped the bike of everything removable—the seat, the handle grips, the reflectors, everything. I pushed a piece of scrap metal home. I had owned that bike one day!

Mother secured a temporary job cleaning a dingy little motel on Lake Travis, which meant that I would go to yet another new school, Leander Elementary School. It was a horrible experience. I remember seeing a kid expose himself to a teacher and to the girls on the bus. I wanted to walk to school to avoid the disgusting pranks on the bus, but it was too far. The kids were terrible. One day a student pushed a teacher into a tall wastebasket. Only her legs and arms hung out; she couldn't move. Everyone else laughed, but I was scared to death. I didn't even know how to tell my mother what was going on. I knew there was nothing she could do about it, and I didn't want to be a tattler. Anyway, she had enough to worry about. More than I knew.

There was another man in her life, one she hadn't even told me about yet.

chapter 3

Cut Off

Aunt Berta was a clerk, and her friend and housemate, Thelma Warren—I called her Timbo—was a schoolteacher. Aunt Berta was a Christian Scientist, and I sometimes went to church with her. Mother and I had visited a few churches when she first took me back, but that was short-lived. I didn't understand anything in the Christian Science church, which may have been fortunate.

Timbo was always good to me. She was my buddy, and I certainly needed one badly. I needed someone to play catch with me, to run with me, to talk with me, to hunt with me. I wanted a daddy and couldn't have one, but I'm a hunter and a conservationist today because Timbo took the time to take me into the woods as a little boy. Somehow, she knew it was in me to want to spend time in the great outdoors.

I saw my first deer with her. It was so beautiful. She guided me to shoot my first dove, too. She always told me not to shoot anything just for the sake of shooting it. "You shoot it either to eat it or as a trophy, never just for the sport of it." One day while we were sitting in the woods, just observing the wildlife, I saw nine doe and a buck walk past, truly an unforgettable sight. Hunting and fishing with her provided some of the most pleasant experiences of my childhood.

I also had a dream. I wanted to grow up to become a great athlete. I didn't care which sport. I was fast and agile and had very unusual athletic ability, but there wasn't much hope for me in organized sports. We moved too frequently, and all the other kids had their daddies to take them to tryouts and to practice with them.

It was impossible to develop any friendships, as often as we moved. I became a timid little guy, dreading everyone's stare as I joined various classrooms in the middle of the year. I became withdrawn and fearful and hardly knew how to talk to people.

The only things I could really look forward to were my birthday and Christmas. Those were the two days in the year when I knew who loved me because they remembered me. Pastor and Mrs. Hale tried to see me on my birthday or at Christmas and take me home with them for a few days. That was like being in heaven, going from one of the run-down places where I lived to a cozy suburban home.

Also on those special days, I'd receive gifts from my adopted brother, Sidney, from Aunt Berta and Timbo, and from Clayton Spriggs—another boy the Hales had taken in as a child. Those gifts made me feel loved. They were the highlights of my year.

During the summer when I was nearly nine, Mother let the Hales take me home with them for a week. I had a great time, and I tried not to think about the circumstances I lived in. The Hales didn't talk about it much, but I learned later that they were heartsick about the conditions and wished they could get me back for good. More than once, they told me later, they considered taking me away from all that and risking the consequences.

After that week of paradise, my mother came to get me. "We're in a new place," she said. I didn't respond. New didn't mean *new*; it just meant different.

I couldn't believe it when I saw it. Our place was just one room, and not a very large one at that. A partition separated the makeshift bathroom from a combination living, sleeping, and eating area. I wanted to ask her if it was really our home, but I couldn't speak. It was in a slum. It was filthy. The people in the neighborhood looked menacing. And then she introduced me to Sam Humphrey, an unemployed man in his sixties, living on a meager social security check.

"I've married this man," she said simply. "He's your stepfather."

I had never seen him before; I hadn't even heard of him. As soon as I got her alone, I said, "Mother, do you know this man? This isn't right."

"Well, son, God told me to marry him, and we just need to be together. He'll help support us, and I can help him get along. He doesn't read or write, so he needs us, too."

I knew it was wrong, even though Mother told me he was a recovering alcoholic who had been converted to Christ. That was okay with me, but marrying him seemed like the dumbest thing she could have done. The only work he ever did was to mow a few lawns once in a while. Three cannot live as cheaply as two; we struggled more than ever.

One day when I was alone in that dingy room we called home, a man knocked on the screen door. I looked up. "Yes, sir?"

He flashed a badge. "I'm a law enforcement officer, son. I've been asked to come and get you and—"

I didn't let him finish. I pretended that I was going to let him in, but instead I shot past him and ran down the street to our landlady's house. I pleaded with her to let me use her phone.

The policeman was close behind, knocking at her door. I called my aunt.

"Aunt Berta! A policeman is trying to take me away!"

"Oh, honey, let him! I called him. I just couldn't stand to see you raised in that place with that man! I had to get you out of there. Go with him, please."

I didn't understand. All I knew was that I didn't want to go anywhere with a policeman. But by the time I got off the phone, he had persuaded the landlady to let him take me. In the car, he told me my aunt had reported that I wasn't getting enough to eat, that I was hungry and needed help.

"That's not true," I said, crying. "I eat balanced meals every day!"

He took me to the detention home in Austin, where I was locked in a room with bars on the windows. I sat there all day, crying, wondering what in the world I had done to wind up in jail. I was cut off from everybody. I didn't know if my mother or stepfather even knew I was there. I knew Aunt Berta knew, so why wasn't she doing something about it?

She *was* doing something. She gave the Hales' name as people who cared about me in the past. The authorities called them, and they immediately drove all the way to Austin to check out my living conditions. It broke their hearts not to be permitted to see me, but they stocked the shelves of our little place and promised to send money regularly for my care. Only then was I released and allowed to go home.

A year later, as I approached my tenth birthday, I couldn't wait to hear from my loved ones. It was the bitterest disappointment of my life when my birthday came and went, unnoticed by anyone but my mother. No gifts. No visits. No cards. No calls. No trips.

I could hardly believe it. They were the only people in the world I loved and trusted not to forget me, yet they had. I was living in the pits, subsisting on Mother's "balanced meals," and despising life. I cried for two days after my birthday, finally resolving never to trust anyone again as long as I lived. If the people I loved couldn't be trusted, who could?

My worst fears would be confirmed over the next several birthdays and Christmases because I didn't hear from or see or receive anything from those people I had depended upon. I didn't learn until much later that none of them, not one, had forgotten me. They had sent greetings and even gifts, but my mother had cut me off from them. Apparently, she was desperate for my love and a relationship with me, and she felt that those others intruded upon that, threatened it.

I was completely devastated. I felt that no one really loved me. No one cared. No one remembered the little boy with no daddy.

I despaired of ever seeing the Hales again. For all I knew, they didn't call, didn't ask to see me, didn't drop in, didn't invite me to their place, and didn't send cards or gifts or anything. Perhaps Mother was as offended at their intrusion in stocking the shelves as she had been at Aunt Berta's calling attention to the problem in the first place. Regardless of the reason, nothing was ever said to me. They simply dropped out of my life, just like everyone else.

When I finally learned the truth years later, I had to fight through my anger toward my mother for being so selfish. I know now that she was just trying to make me love her. But she went about it the wrong way, and she nearly ruined her little boy's mind. I realize that she didn't know any better. I now forgive her completely.

At the time I was so despondent, felt so worthless, that many nights I cried and cried. I figured I was a bad boy, and that must be why I never got any breaks. No dad. No friends. No sports to play. No loved ones who remembered me. Sometimes, when I was home alone, I banged my head against the wall until I knocked myself out. I just wanted to escape. I was one miserable little boy.

Over the next few years, as we moved to the back side of a garbage dump, into an alley, and to the rears of many a house, my mother's inconsistencies began to show. She had been thrilled with my stepfather's testimony, how he had been saved from alcoholism, and she talked often of how God told her I would bring joy to the world. But she didn't read the Bible. She put down the church and people who went there, and we seldom, if ever, attended.

Suddenly she got it in her head, when I was about twelve, that I should be christened in a church. It sounded all right to me. I didn't know what it meant, but I had been getting enough confused signals about God all my life that I was sufficiently intrigued to keep my ears and eyes open in case there was anything in it for me. Nothing else had added much to my life.

I was christened at a big Episcopal church in downtown Austin, which gave Mother some sort of comfort. It didn't mean anything to me. In the Episcopal Sunday school, I discovered that the people didn't think or act any differently from us. Eventually, Mother stopped requiring that I go. (Since that time I have met fine, Spirit-filled believers in Episcopal churches.)

When I think back on our sad existence, I remember no birds, flowers, sunsets, sunrises, or beautiful days. The memories of seeing wildlife in the woods with Timbo Warren faded quickly as I was cut off from loved ones, and I lived just to get by. I had nothing in life to enjoy or appreciate. My stepfather was pretty much a silent partner, not a mean person, just illiterate and quiet. I soon realized that he was simply one man doing his best.

When more than two years had passed since I'd heard anything from my loved ones, I nearly gave up hope. My frame of mind was woeful. I knew, beyond a shadow of a doubt, that I was worthless. Mother wouldn't let me try out for football in junior high. That was one sport I know I could have truly excelled at. I was big and rangy, tough enough to take on anyone. It would have perfectly fit my personality. I could have hidden in that helmet and crushed people, taking out my frustrations on them. But no. Mother strictly prohibited that. It was too bad, too. The upper-class kids played football. The others had street fights.

When I went to try out for organized baseball, it seemed that everyone else had his dad with him. They played catch, ran, hit, shagged fly balls, and registered. Again I was embarrassed that I didn't even know what to put on the card for family information. My name was Robison. My birth certificate said Wattinger. My parents' name was Humphrey.

I was nervous and felt conspicuous, but I really wanted to do my best. I hit every ball thrown to me and caught everything hit to me. I ran like the wind. I could hear the appreciative sounds and whistles from the other players and the coaches. I couldn't wait to see what team I would be on and whether we would get uniforms.

After the tryouts, the kids gathered around to find out what would happen. The guy in charge explained that the coaches had rated the players in various categories, and they were going to be assigned some paper chips with which they would bid for and "buy" the players of their choice.

I had done well. They knew who I was. But all of a sudden I was petrified. Too much was against me. Common sense should have told me that it didn't matter that my daddy wasn't there. It didn't matter that I was new, or quiet, or shy, or withdrawn, or skinny, or poor. But it mattered to me. I simply wouldn't be able to take it if, for some reason, they overlooked me.

What if they all knew each other and wanted their friends on their teams? What if there were favors to dole out before they got to unknowns like me? I had to get out of there. I couldn't stay. I just couldn't. How would I be able to bear hearing the names called out, finding that several dozen kids' names would be called before mine? What if they had lost mine or couldn't read the name? Who would stick up for me? What dad would say, "Now, see here! What about my son James, the one who did so well?"

As the kids milled about, waiting for the coaches to make their choices, I slipped away. I ran home, crying, knowing down deep that I had as much talent and ability as anyone there, but also knowing that I simply couldn't take being overlooked, not again.

A Reunion

Mother let me get a job where I stood from noon to early evening sacking groceries. Although I was able to save a little money—I wanted a motor scooter—the job didn't add to my self-confidence. I was low man on the totem pole and wouldn't speak to anyone. I was a very shy, withdrawn boy. My body was changing, my voice was getting lower, and I felt ugly and worthless. Pictures from back then tell a different story. My friends say there was a dark handsomeness about the thin face and the deep-set eyes, but we are what we think we are. I thought I was nothing. Even my sprinting ability diminished because the work I was doing tightened my leg muscles instead of keeping them lithe.

One of our more than a dozen moves found us in the first house we'd been in, one with two bedrooms. Mother and Sam slept in the dining room. I had my own room, and in the bedroom next to mine was an elderly woman whom my mother, as a practical nurse, cared for. One night the woman died. I had known her, spoken to her, seen her every day. She wasn't related to me, but it was spooky to lose someone I had known. The ambulance came, there was a lot of commotion, and I realized that she had died in the room next to mine while I was there. It was not a good experience for a painfully shy young teen. I knew enough to know that the woman's meager home care payment was helping keep us alive. And now she was gone. We would soon lose the house.

Mother and Sam's marriage was on the rocks. I heard a lot of talk about my real father, Joe Bailey Robison, from my mother and other relatives. Apparently, he still lived in the area. I was curious about him and had a vague memory of maybe seeing him once or twice when I was a child, but I didn't know if I wanted to see him again or not.

I couldn't have been more miserable. I was sullen and independent, and my mother didn't know what to do with me while she and Sam looked for another place to live. For years I hadn't heard from or seen anyone who used to love me. With all the moving, the disappointments, and the end of all my dreams, I felt like I was going nowhere.

Maybe my mother was more sensitive than I thought. She realized she had to do something with me. Out of the blue one Sunday afternoon, she asked me if I wanted to call the Hales and see if they wanted me to visit for a week. I almost burst into tears.

I poured money into a pay phone, my hands trembling as I dialed. I hadn't spoken to them in years. What if they didn't want to see me, or even talk to me? How could I know? I wouldn't even know what to call whoever answered the phone. Mrs. Hale? Mama? Daddy? Pastor Hale? It rang and rang. Finally, Daddy Hale answered. "Hello! Preacher, Preacher Daddy? This is James!"

There was a long silence. I held my breath. Then I heard him sob. "Mama, go to the other phone," he said, his voice thick. "It's James!" And he broke down again.

"James?" Mama asked.

"Yes, Mama, it's me." We were all crying. They managed questions about how I was, where I was, what was the matter, everything. But between each question and answer, we blubbered so much we could hardly understand each other.

The operator cut in. "Three minutes, signal when through, please."

"But, ma'am," I said, "we ain't done nothin' but cry so far."

"Signal when through, please."

"Son," Daddy Hale said, "We waited so long to hear from you."

"Listen," I said quickly, "Mother says I can come to see you if you will get me and have me home by a week from tomorrow."

They wept some more. "I have to preach the evening service tonight, James, but we'll be there for you tomorrow morning. You sure it's all right?"

"Yes, sir!"

I hardly slept. They arrived early the next morning, and their car looked like a chariot coming for me. I sat in the back seat of the car, pretending that I was a little boy again and that I had a family, a mom and a dad who loved me and raised me in a nice house.

That night I saw tile in a bathroom for the first time. Their little two-bedroom house looked like a mansion to me. Normally I had trouble getting to sleep. That night, knowing I would be there a week, I fell asleep almost instantly. I felt secure.

I felt loved that whole week. Young people from the church came by, and we went out and did things together. They seemed to like me, even though I barely spoke two words to anyone. I just drank it all in. I was still so timid that I couldn't carry on a conversation, but I enjoyed myself immensely. The only thing I dreaded was Sunday school and church the next Sunday. I had no interest, no reason to go, but I knew I couldn't get out of it. I would have to tell my name and where I was from, and everyone would make a big fuss over me because I was staying with the Hales.

Sunday morning was barely tolerable, and I thought I'd caught a bit of a break that evening. Mrs. Hale told me I could stay home and watch television when they went to the preservice training union Bible study, and then she would come back and get me for the evening meeting. That sounded great. I didn't want to go home the next day, and maybe the variety would make the time move more slowly.

But I didn't know that Mrs. Hale would go to church and interrupt every department's Bible study. With tears streaming down her face, she asked them to set aside their study for that night and get on their knees and pray for me. "You know James, the little boy we raised until he was five? We hadn't seen him for years, and he's here with us this week. He's going home tomorrow, and we don't know if we'll ever see him again. Pray that he'll receive Jesus tonight. Pray God will save him."

All over the Memorial Baptist church in Pasadena, Texas, that night in 1957, hundreds of people went to their knees. While I sat in the parsonage idly watching television, spiritual warfare was being waged for my soul. I had no idea when she came to pick me up that I would arrive at a church saturated with the presence of God. The lower auditorium was filling up. All five hundred theater-type seats would be taken. When Mama Hale led me to the end of one row, I wasn't aware that she was trying to make it easy for me to go forward if I made a decision.

After the singing and the preliminaries, Pastor Hale announced that he wasn't going to preach. "I want our young people to stand and tell us what Jesus means to them. Who would like to start us off?"

Good, I thought. *This won't take long. Young people won't want to say anything about Jesus.* But all around me, young people were standing. I turned and craned my neck. All over the auditorium young people were standing! Many were the very kids who had befriended me during the week, who had accepted the quiet visitor and didn't make him feel like an outsider.

Pastor Hale laughed. "I can see we're going to have to do this one at a time," he said. "As I call on you, come to the microphone and testify."

The testimonies were so real and so heartfelt that I was stunned. This was no fake deal. The kids meant business. Jesus was real to them. He was life to them. They had something I didn't have, and the more I listened, the more troubled I became. I couldn't hold back the tears. I slouched in my seat, my face in my hand, trying to hide that I was crying.

Finally, after almost an hour, it was mercifully over. We stood to sing, but God was still dealing with me. I could sense His Spirit talking to mine. "You've always wanted a father, James. Let Me be your Father. You've always wanted a family. Let My children be your family."

Daddy Hale stood at the front, inviting anyone who wanted to "give your life to Jesus, to come down here and take me by the hand." I knew I needed Jesus. I knew it as clearly as I had ever known anything. But I couldn't go forward in front of people. I was too shy. I grabbed the back of the chair in front of me and held on tight. I stared at the floor but sensed someone was coming toward me.

It was Mama Hale. She put her hand on my shoulder, and I looked into her face. Tears were flowing out from under her glasses. "James," she said. "Don't you want to go to Jesus?"

"Yes, ma'am, but I'm afraid."

"I'll go with you. We can go together."

I stepped out into the aisle with her, a scared teenage boy with no home, no real family, no future, no hope. The boy who couldn't give a report in class walked down the aisle in front of more than five hundred people to give his heart to Jesus.

I remembered having recently read a Classic Comics Book on the life of Christ and being impressed when Jesus was baptized and God said, "This is My beloved Son, in whom I am well pleased." I thought how nice it was that Jesus had a Father who was pleased with Him. I never had a daddy who told me, "Nice catch; way to go; nice hit; good boy; I'm pleased."

But when I put my hand in the pastor's hand, I put my life in the hand of God. And it was as if I could hear Him saying, "This is James, My beloved son, in whom I am well pleased. Way to go, James. Nice hit; nice catch; good going!"

I prayed and told God that I knew I was a sinner in need of a Savior. I turned over everything I knew of myself to everything I knew of Him and said, "God, save me." And I knew He had. I was still shy and withdrawn, but when asked if I wanted to express my salvation publicly through the waters of baptism, I immediately agreed. When it was all over and I was shaking hands with many people, I realized my clothes were dry. What had I changed into? Mama Hale had been so confident that her prayers, and the prayers of the congregation, would be answered, she had brought a change of clothes for me.

I returned to Austin to yet another squalid living arrangement, but one thing was different. Mother had divorced Sam Humphrey. It was just the two of us again.

"Mother," I announced, "I got saved last night."

She laughed at me. "When God gets ready to save you, He'll let me know."

I was crushed. "Mother, I really got saved."

She didn't respond.

At first, I was on fire for God. By Tuesday, I had led my one friend, Charles Alexander, to Christ simply by telling him what Jesus had done for me. He and his mother were also victims of an alcoholic father who was long gone. Charles got as excited as I was. We spent Thursday night out under the stars in the woods behind our place. We had a great time, howling when the tent fell on Charles's head. I told him, "Just sit that way all night, buddy! You're holdin' the tent up!" We laughed till we cried.

We talked and talked about how we didn't have fathers at home. "But we both have the same heavenly Father, don't we, Charles?" We prayed together for hours, singing and laughing. It was a special night when two young boys, waifs in the world, exulted in the fact that their Father had made the universe.

With more moves and more trauma in my life, I lost track of my first convert. I haven't seen or heard from Charles Alexander in thirty years.

I didn't really know how to walk with God because I couldn't find a church like Memorial Baptist. I tried a few, but people looked right through me. Maybe my clothes were too ragged, or I looked too shy. I think the main problem was that the churches were dead. I was in love with Jesus, but no one at those churches seemed to be.

Shortly, I drifted from church, and from God. I drifted, but He didn't. He was closer to me than He had been before I became a Christian, of course. I thought He had been watching over me since my childhood, such as the time my heart stopped beating after I had shrugged Him off. I had no idea how clearly He would speak to me now that I was one of His.

By the time I got into the tenth grade, I had saved enough for a motor scooter and was becoming something of a ladies' man. I wasn't much for chatting with people or meeting new friends, but I learned to come on to the girls. I wasn't terrible, but I wasn't nice either. My intentions were not pure, and thankfully I was never as successful as I hoped to be.

I was making a major move on one girl, and my mother knew I was up to no good. I got ready to see the girl one day and knew that I shouldn't. I had no good on my mind, and my conscience was working on me. I fired up my scooter and said, "Mother, I'll see you."

She didn't even know what I was up to, but she knew where I was going. For some reason she looked me dead in the eye and said, "You ought not to go."

I knew she was right. It was as if her words had come straight from God, as if He were telling me in my heart, "You ought not to go." I knew it. She knew it. He knew it. I had been in this position before. I had shrugged off the warning then, and I was going to shrug it off now.

I looked back at her and said, "Shoot."

"You ought to stay here today, son."

"No, I'm going."

"Well, good-by, playboy."

That stunned me. She wasn't using the term the way it's used today. She was just implying that all I wanted to do was to play, to do what I wanted to do and nothing else. God was speaking to me through her, just like the Scriptures say He does.

Still, I laughed at her and rode off. God said to me again, "You ought not to go."

And just as definitely, I said to myself, "I'll do what I want to do."

Soon I would realize that those were words I would regret for a long time.

"That's Your Daddy"

At fourteen, I was just barely old enough to ride the scooter. I had a reputation for safety, and I was doing the speed limit. There's something about trying to ignore the working of the Spirit of God in your conscience, though, that makes you preoccupied. I had no idea trouble was ahead.

I had been doing a little over forty miles an hour for more than a mile when I came very close to a car and followed it too closely into the busy Austin intersection of LeMar Avenue and Twenty-fourth Street. When that car signaled a left, I swung around it to the right without slowing down to proceed through the intersection. The seconds I was behind that car apparently blocked me from the view of the driver of a car coming from the other direction. He turned left without knowing that I was speeding toward him in the outer lane.

I couldn't see him either. One instant I was tooling through the intersection at forty miles an hour, and the next I was ten feet from a car looming directly before me. I reacted instinctively, jerking the wheel of the scooter to the left to get out of the car's way. I flung my body weight to the left, too, to put the scooter into a slide that would stop it or at least slow it down enough to miss the car.

As if in slow motion, I wrestled that scooter to the ground and heard the sickening scrape and crunch of metal on pavement as I continued to slide toward the car. The leg underneath me absorbed all the damage; it was torn open to the bone as I whipped over that rough concrete. I was heading straight for the door of the passenger side of the car. If my head hit that door, I knew it would be crushed by the impact. I'd never survive.

Somehow, in that millisecond I was aware that the driver of the vehicle must have known the same thing. Rather than hit the brake, as would most people seeing a motor scooter sliding toward them, the driver gunned his engine. His maneuver worked!

Instead of hitting the door, my scooter and I slammed into the finder behind the back wheel. Whaamm!! The impact of the scooter hitting the fender tore the back of the car away from the body. I continued end over end through the pathway between the main body of the car and the severed piece, just as Moses and the Israelites moved through the parted Red Sea. The car slid to the curb, and I wound up in a crouched position, a bloody mess. My scooter was mangled. The car was half ripped apart. I felt a dozen pairs of eyes on me as pedestrians gathered with motorists to see if I was alive.

My jeans were already stuck to the blood oozing from the deep wound in my leg. I couldn't move without a searing pain caused by the ripping of the muscle and tissue. Having those jeans removed later would be as painful as the initial impact, and seeing the extent of the damage nearly made me pass out.

I craned my neck to look again for the driver. He sat in his car, talking on a radio. It turned out he was a deputy sheriff. After he called an ambulance, he hurried over to me. He was a big, strong man, and he looked worried. "You did good, son. I knew if I didn't speed up, you were a dead man, so I tried to get out of your way. I didn't quite make it, son, but you did good."

My leg was torn to the bone, and the muscles were compressed terribly, to the point that I still feel some pain in them to this day. Miraculously, the bones were not broken, and except for a lot of scrapes and bruises, I painfully survived. I was off my feet for a couple of weeks, and that deputy sheriff visited me every week. He kept complimenting me on how well I had handled myself and my scooter. The truth was, he had saved my life by speeding up.

Down deep I knew that while God had spared my life, He had allowed that accident because of my willful disobedience. I had known good and well that He had said I ought not to go to that girl's house, having in mind what I had in mind. During my mending process, He impressed deep upon my heart, "Things are going to be different between you and Me now, James. You don't go your own way anymore. I am your Father. You will be corrected when you take issue!"

After a long rehabilitation, I went back to work and tried to put a few dollars aside for the first time in my life. The total amount was less than twenty dollars, but it gave me a feeling of security to have a little savings.

The insurance company paid to fix my scooter, but I didn't want to ride it again as long as I lived. I sold it and spent the money on a beautiful one-hundred-dollar rifle and scope, a Model 70, long-barrel, 30.06 Winchester, which—along with all such pre-1964 models—has become a classic. I still have it, and it's very valuable, especially since I've kept it in mint condition. My mother wondered why I wanted it because we were not near anywhere I could shoot it. I just thought it was beautiful. I knew someday I would get to go hunting and use it.

Several months after the accident, I fell as ill as I'd ever been. I had a case of strep throat that acted as if it wanted to kill me. The infection got so bad that I developed a high fever; I was delirious, hallucinating and screaming with pain. Mother took my temperature frequently and later told me that it rose sharply. stayed in the 104 and 105 range for several hours, and then shot up even higher. She could hardly believe her eyes when the thermometer showed 108 degrees. As a practical nurse, she knew that if the thing was even close to accurate, she absolutely had to get my temperature down.

She filled the bathtub with cold water and as many ice cubes as possible. It was all she could do to get her strapping son in there. I cried and hollered, and when my temperature dropped only a degree or two, she knew she was going to have to swallow her pride and ask for help. It wasn't that she didn't want a doctor; she couldn't afford one.

Somehow, she persuaded one to come as an act of mercy. He checked me over quickly, pumped me full of penicillin, and told my mother, "If you hadn't called me when you did, you'd have lost this boy. He ought to be in a hospital right now."

Mother told the doctor she simply couldn't afford to hospitalize me, and he gave her prescriptions for more penicillin. Later, I heard her on the phone to Joe Bailey Robison. "If you want to see your son alive, you'd better get over here." Get over here? My *daddy?* No warning? No preparation? Would he come? What would I say? What would I do? I didn't know whether to dread it or look forward to it.

The next day, as I lay on the couch in the living room, I heard a car pull up out front. My mother came over to me and helped me sit up so I could look out the window. "Son, that's your daddy."

I saw a car parked right in the middle of the street. For drivers to get around it from either direction, they would have to drive up on the parkway. Emerging from the car was a tall man, over six two, with wavy black hair. *Boy, he's big*, I thought. *Maybe he'll play ball with me outside sometime. We can play catch with the football.*

He staggered up the walk and up the steps, and my mother made an awkward introduction. My long-lost father hardly looked at me. I quickly realized that he was sober. He walked like a drunk even when he wasn't drunk, and because his gait looked so funny, I never wanted any friends to see him.

I wouldn't have dreamed of hugging him. I was afraid of him. He didn't look particularly boisterous, and it was clear that my mother was partial to him, even after all he'd put her through. When he moved in, I thought she was just letting him stay with us a few days because I was sick and she needed help. Soon it looked permanent.

As I gained my strength, I became well enough to go outside. I asked him to throw the football with me. He said sure and lurched out behind me. I threw it to him. He made an awkward gesture to snatch it with stiff arms and stone hands. I decided he was just rusty. When he tried to throw the ball to me, though, I knew how hopeless it was. He gripped the ball by one end, causing it to flip end over end when he threw it.

And his first past was his best. I told him I'd thrown enough and wanted to do something else. He was pitiful. What kind of a dad was he? A few nights later, I found out.

He came home drunk, in a rage. I was scared to death of him. I had seen drunk people before, but never this close. He cursed my mother and me. I hated his talking ugly like that, and I knew he was dangerous. I didn't want to be around him. I didn't want to see him again. And I certainly didn't want to be like him.

I couldn't believe it a few weeks later when he was sober for three straight days. Mother must have made it a prerequisite, because the next thing I knew, she announced to me that they were going to be married. She actually acted as if that would please me. "You'll have your mama and daddy together with you in the same house, finally."

I was speechless. *Yeah,* I thought. *It's not even our house.*

I couldn't know that Mother would divorce and remarry him again several times over the next few years. She needed security like anyone else, and I guess she thought the father of her child was as good as any man. She was always optimistic or naive enough to believe his promises when he'd vow to quit drinking.

Our lives became a living hell. I repented of all the times I wished I had a daddy who would join our family. We were so much better off without him that I can't even describe the difference. "Life with father" became one miserable experience after the other.

It wasn't long before my tiny savings disappeared. Of course, neither Mother or Daddy Joe, as I called him, had any idea where it could have gone. I believed Mother. As for Daddy, I was fairly certain it went into his gut. My Fitch Hair Tonic bottle went from half full one night to empty the next morning. Mother claimed that her vinegar and even her cooking oil were running out faster than normal. The hair tonic I could understand; it had alcohol in it. But the man hoarded, hid, and drank everything in the house. Alcohol or not, if it was liquid, he considered it his. He couldn't throw a pass or hit a baseball. He did only one thing well. Drink.

Sometimes he made me go with him when he visited other women in their homes. I waited in the car while he committed adultery, and he would brag about it all the way home as he swore me to secrecy. I despised him.

The only thing that surprised me about him—and it certainly wasn't much of a redeeming factor—was that he could play the piano and sing fairly well. Years later I would dream of the day when my daddy would get saved, come and testify at one of my crusades, and then play and sing for the crowd. But it never happened.

One night I came home, and my mother was crying and holding her throat. "What's the matter, Mama?"

She could hardly speak. "Your daddy came home drunk and cursed me, and I must've said something that set him off."

"Why?"

She waved a hand of dismissal as if she didn't want to talk about it. Her eyes were red and teary.

I pressed her. "What did he do?"

"He choked me. If I hadn't fainted and dropped to the floor, I know he would have killed me. He left me for dead, but I came to later."

I was trembling with rage, and I wanted to say that I would kill him, I would avenge her, I would even the score. But the story scared the fire out of me. What would I have done if she had died? I couldn't survive without her. And I couldn't fight him unless I caught him asleep or off guard. No way I could stand up to that big man.

A few nights later, after he had been gone for three or four days, I was faced with the opportunity. He came barreling into the house, probably looking to curse my mother. When he spied me, he lit into me. He yelled and cursed and ranted and raved. "I'm goin' to kill you, boy!"

I believed him. It was time to do something, to put up or shut up. I knew I was no match for him, drunk or sober, but I wasn't going to stand there and let him kill me.

I kept my peace until he dropped heavily into a chair. He sat there cursing and threatening, but I knew as long as he stayed in that chair, he couldn't get to me. The problem was, he was sitting between me and the door, the only way of escape. His eyes were afire and unfocused. I ran to the other room and grabbed a baseball bat, wildly looking behind me to see if he was following. He wasn't. I could hear him mumbling. He sounded as if he was still in the chair.

I could go back out with the bat and confront him, but what if he overpowered me? That would work only if he was still in the chair, and I had no way of knowing that. If I came out with the bat, he might charge me and kill me before I could do anything. Once he was on his feet, a bat would be useless unless I got lucky. I listened again. It still sounded as if he was in the chair, spewing verbal assaults.

I ran to the closet and reached for my Winchester 30.06. Hands trembling, heart blasting away, I dug in a drawer for a box of high-powered expanding bullets. I'd seen them demonstrated. A man shot at a tree from fifty feet and nearly blew it down. It cut a huge hole in the trunk, even from that distance.

I jammed a shell into the chamber and snapped the weapon shut. Sweating, shivering, and wondering if I would wake up the next morning, I crept out into the living room and stood a few paces from my daddy, leveling the rifle at him. He cursed me with every breath, still promising to kill me.

"If you get up," I said, my voice choked with emotion, "If you so much as move, I'll blow a hole in you big enough to crawl through. Don't think I won't. Don't test me, 'cause I'll do it, I swear I will. You don't come around here chokin' my mother and sayin' you're gonna kill me. No, sir."

"I'm gonna kill you, boy!"

I had never felt so alone, so helpless and hopeless. And the man who gave me life was sitting right there in front of me. My finger curled tighter around the trigger. "You so much as move your arm, I'll kill you."

How he could yell and scream and swear and threaten so loud without moving puzzles me to this day. I watched him for the slightest movement. I was ready to fire, and from that distance, I'd have blown him and his chair right back through the wall.

How I kept from firing when I saw a figure appear at the door, I don't know. There was a loud knock, and a voice bigger, stronger, and more piercing than Daddy's filled the room. When the figure entered, Daddy lurched around in his chair to see who it was.

My arms felt like lead.

Betty

I released my finger from the trigger and slumped to the floor when I realized our intruder was the deputy sheriff who had saved my life in the motor scooter accident. This time he saved my daddy's life, and he saved me from a miserable future, having to live with the killing of my own father.

Daddy was arrested and taken to jail, where he would stay for several weeks. When he got out, he wrote some bad checks and wound up in jail again. Over the next several years he would be in and out of jails and state institutions, generally making life impossible for my mother.

She lost her job and her home, and she didn't know what to do with me. The end of tenth grade had come, and I begged her to let me go to the Hales' home for the summer. She agreed, and so did they. I didn't know when I left her that I would not be coming back, except to visit and pick up my belongings. I just knew I wanted a summer break from the madness my father had created.

I knew I'd have to go to church with the Hales, but I figured I could endure that. I was trying to behave myself, except in the girl department, and though I hadn't slept with anyone, I would have if I'd had the right chance. I did whatever else I could get away with, and finding more prospects was always on my mind. The only things my cronies and I in Austin seemed to talk about was making out with girls. I thought that was life itself, and I looked forward to all the good-looking girls in the Houston area. I was fifteen years old.

There were nice girls around, too; I had seen them in high school, but I couldn't touch them with a ten-foot pole. That was the kind of girl I truly wanted, but I didn't really know any. I may have been smooth with the girls who let themselves be hustled, but otherwise, I was an extremely shy, self-conscious, withdrawn, and unhappy young man.

I hated social situations, and I hated church. I immediately immersed myself in the church softball team in Pasadena that summer, where I could excel, take a few compliments, and then busy myself with just playing when the spotlight got too bright. I did prove that summer, though, that I would have been a good baseball player if I had been given the chance.

In the youth meetings I stayed in the background. Man, if anybody had asked me to lead in prayer, I think I'd have died. They liked to pass around the chores of making announcements and giving testimonies and such, but I made it very clear with my silence, slouching, and lack of eye contact that I wasn't interested in doing any of those things. That wasn't my scene. I wasn't ugly about it. I was just determined to stay out of the limelight—no matter what.

I could identify with all the research that would come along years later and say that most people's greatest fear is public speaking. I didn't so much as answer an easy question in a Sunday school class, a youth meeting, or a training union Bible study group. My role was secure. I was a silent partner, and that's the way I liked it. In fact, that's the way I demanded it. If someone had tried to change it, I would have left. No question.

The only activity that really interested me was checking out the girls. Who was available and willing, and who wasn't? Like I say, down deep I wanted a nice, innocent, pretty Christian one. But that was for later. That was for a lifetime. When I got around to choosing a spouse, I wanted a princess. But to mess around with, to have some not-so-nice fun, that was a different story. In church, you should be able to tell which are which, but I wasn't too good at that yet. I assumed they were all easy, the way they had been in Austin. So I just kept my eye on the cutest ones and hoped for the best.

I had never actually been on a date. Of course, Mother didn't have a car, and Daddy—when he was around—wouldn't let me drive his without a license. When I tried to hustle a girl, I just showed up at her house and tried my moves on her. But when I tried that in Pasadena with the church girls, I didn't get any-where.

Then it happened. Sitting in the back row of the training union study one Sunday night, I was slouching and acting cool as usual when for some reason a little brown-haired girl with green eyes turned around and smiled at me. That wiped me out. She was petite, about five three with a great figure, and she was the cutest little bobby soxer I had ever seen. And that smile! I didn't know a girl could get to me like that.

I watched her and soon realized that she, like me, was athletic and outdoorsy. Then I found out that she had signed up to work in Vacation Bible School that summer. I was the farthest thing from spiritual, but suddenly I decided that I would work with the children in VBS. In truth, I would be working on the girl with the smile. Betty Freeman.

She had dated some of the most popular guys in the local high school, one an all-state football player, and I should have realized that she was only interested in me because I was a challenge. She thought I was cute, but she also knew I was shy and withdrawn, and maybe she thought she could draw me out a little.

I followed her around and flirted with her all during VBS. She thought I was fun and nice, and I was hoping she wasn't—nice, that is. She was so sweet, I should have known better, though. Finally, I mustered my courage and asked her out. It was to be just a-burger-and-a-Coke date, but I had to talk Daddy Hale into letting me use his car, even though I was underage. I think because he and Mama Hale knew how sweet Betty was, they thought it would be worth the risk to let me go out with her. Had they only known!

We got a bite to eat and then drove around. I pretended to be lost, and before I knew it, I *was*. I wound up behind a school and suggested we just sit there and talk. She may have been naive and inexperienced, but I learned later that I hadn't fooled her in the least. She wondered what in the world this guy was doing, a guy living with a preacher wanting to park on a first date!

I started talking to her about how experienced I was romantically and how I had been wondering what she liked to do or not do. It was inappropriate, to say the least, and I was forthright to a fault. She was shocked, hardly able to answer my crude questions. What she did say made me think she was the dumbest girl I'd ever met, at least in the area of romance. I leaned over and kissed her.

I tried talking to her some more, attempting to find out if she had any experience at all. When it was clear she didn't, I thought I'd really hit the big time, stealing a kiss on the first date with a girl who wasn't used to that. I stole another and told her it was time to go home. I drove to her place and stopped out front. She waited—I know now she was waiting for me to get

50

out and open the door for her, but I had never had a date before, had never driven a girl anywhere—and I just sat there looking at her. Finally, she got out and walked to the door alone as I drove away. I didn't even wait until she was safely inside. She had to think I was the dumbest clod on earth.

As soon as I was out of her sight, something strange happened. I began to cry. It was hard to drive with tears stinging my eyes. When I pulled into the Hales' driveway, I wiped my face and summoned my most composed look to get me past their questions.

They wanted to know how it went, how I liked her, and if I would see her again. I sped through the answers and begged off to go to bed. As soon as I got to my room, the tears began again, and I found myself sobbing as I dropped to my knees. I wasn't a half-spiritual teenager, but I prayed for the first time in a long time.

"Dear God, thank You that I met a pure girl who doesn't know anything ugly." My opinion of her had changed in an instant. I went from being amused by her naivety to being overwhelmed by her sweetness and innocence. I didn't know what the future held, but I knew I wanted to be part of hers.

When I recall that date, it isn't hard to understand why Betty didn't like me at first. I liked her a whole lot more than she liked me, and I kept asking her out. She accepted, but she seemed indifferent.

I met her family. She was the third of four children. Her brother was the oldest and the only boy. He was popular and a good athlete. Her sister was smart, but Betty—though intelligent—didn't like school that much and did just enough to get by. Her little sister was the baby. So Betty was just Betty. Not a boy. Not the smartest. Not the baby.

Of course, I was too young to put all that together and realize that she might battle a lifelong self-image problem. I just knew I liked her and wanted to keep dating her. She wasn't much more spiritual than I was—and that wasn't much—so I didn't feel the pressure I might have if she had been on fire for God all that time. I knew I was a Christian, but witnessing or testifying, man, that was for someone else. I would play church basketball or softball, and I had fun with our own group of kids, but that was the extent of it.

After a couple of months of going with Betty, I wanted to go steady. Her family planned a brief vacation to Lufkin, about a hundred miles away, and I saw her off with a small gift and a request. I should have known how the request was going to go over when she barely acknowledged the gift; maybe she knew what was coming.

"I want you to go with me, Betty."

"You mean go steady? No, I'm not going steady."

That made me mad. I said, "I'll tell you what, if I tell you that I'm not going to go with anybody else, then that's how it's going to be with you. You're not going to go with anyone else."

She shook her head.

"All right then," I said. "If that's not how it's going to be, it ain't goin' to be nothin'."

She left under that tension, and I was sad. Clearly, she didn't care for me the way I cared for her, and I was sure she would date around on her vacation and come back with let's-be-friends news.

She told me later that she got to Lufkin and started flirting with guys and going out with a few. But suddenly, they didn't appeal to her, and she thought about me all the time. I knew something was up when she came back. She told me she had been thinking about it and she had decided to go steady with me after all. By the time school started in the fall, we were an item.

I told my mother I wanted to stay in Pasadena, with the Hales, and I suppose it was a relief to her. She would be marrying and divorcing my father every few months, moving from place to place and from job to job. She missed me and I visited her as often as I could, but I know it had to be a comfort to her not to have to worry about me.

Once we started going steady, Betty had more affection for me than I had for her. Since I had been so lovesick when I wasn't sure how she felt, she must have been puzzled that after she agreed to go steady, she was more into the relationship than I was.

Going together provided a lot of security for both of us. I cleaned up my roving act, and we could hide in our partnership. We never thought twice about whether we would attend certain functions, including church and socials, as a couple. And she was so sweet and friendly, I could hang in the background like I wanted. Only Betty and a few friends ever saw the "real" me. I couldn't, wouldn't, speak up in a social setting. Too painful. Too much attention. Too many chances to misspeak, to show my ignorance, to make a fool of myself.

Besides, I was nobody from nowhere. I had no background, no kind of family worth talking about. I had never been anywhere or done anything, and I certainly wasn't a model Christian. The only thing I had going for me was my steady, Betty Freeman, the sweetest and cutest girl around. I knew she was thinking about marriage soon after we graduated from high school, but I wasn't so sure about rushing into that.

I was comfortable with her, I had a job helping the pipefitters and insulators at a local plant, and I figured I'd just take life as it came. It felt so good to be out of the grim circumstances I had grown up in, to have a steady girl, loving foster parents, and a nice church where I was able to hide without being too committed. And I was able to be an athlete of sorts. During my junior and senior years in high school, I played all kinds of sports for the school and the church.

We had four consensus all-Americans in our church basket-ball league, yet I led the conference in scoring, averaging in the high 20s per game. Eventually, the scouts who came to watch the games discovered me and offered scholarships. That kind of attention was new and exciting to me. But something was coming that would turn my head even further.

My future was not to be in college or professional athletics. It was to be in an area that no one who knew me would have imagined.

Called

During the summer of 1961, after I had graduated from high school at the age of seventeen, I worked as a craftsman's helper on a crew that did pipefitting and insulating of pipes wherever there was a new chemical plant or refinery. That summer, we worked steadily at the PetroTex Chemical Company where a new branch was being built.

If I had a long-term goal, it was to become a professional person, maybe a lawyer, so I wouldn't have to live in poverty like my mother had. I had to make good money and save it with a vengeance. Meanwhile, I was dating Betty and enjoying sports in the church and industrial leagues.

At the end of the summer, in August, my friends pulled a dirty trick on me. They planned a youth-led revival and invited Daniel Vestal, a sixteen-year-old phenomenon to preach at our church. The young people would be in charge of the whole thing. I kept a respectful distance, and based on my record, no one would have bet I would even show up. Well, Betty might have been able to drag me out for a night or two, but that wasn't going to be my scene. Enter, the dirty trick.

One night at youth group, they decided to elect the committee to head the thing up, and first off they nominated me for youth pastor. I was almost too embarrassed to decline, it was so stupid, so ludicrous. Everybody howled. I said, "No. No. Forget it." I was smiling, but they could tell I was not at all pleased that they had made me speak up.

It was a setup. There were no other nominations. My declining was ignored. I was elected unanimously. Some of the kids laughed so hard imagining what ol' clod kicker Robison would do in such a role that they could hardly vote. When it was all over, I was mad. I could have just told them what I thought of them and stomped out, but it became a matter of pride. I had to call their bluff. Take the job. Do the best I could.

"What do I hafta do?" I muttered.

They explained that I would host Daniel Vestal. I would drive him around, take him to eat, spend time with him, sit on the platform, and introduce him every night. I could handle all of it until they got to that platform and introducing part. They could see me turn colors, and the snickering continued. Betty looked at me as if she knew I could do it if I tried. I was in a corner. I couldn't chicken out.

I dreaded the assignment all summer. Worst of all, I knew I didn't love the Lord with all my heart. Betty and I went through the motions, but we were pretty much floating along. At work I sat around the flatbed trucks at lunchtime with a few hundred other guys, listening to the dirty stories and the swearing. I didn't do it, but it didn't faze me much either.

I was nervous about having to hang around a spiritual guy like Daniel Vestal. What would he be like? And what would he expect of a youth pastor? I knew I'd have to do some big-league faking. But the idea of introducing him, of sitting up on the platform with him and having to get up and say something made me wish I'd come down with some debilitating disease.

Daniel, who would grow up to become a powerful Southern Baptist preacher, pastor of the First Baptist Church of Midland, Texas, was wonderful. He treated me great and included me in everything. His behavior was convicting. He assumed that I cared about souls the way he did and that I would be eager to agonize in prayer with him over the lost. I tried, but I knew I was being phony.

I cared more about where we would eat and what time I would take him to the church than I did about the purpose of the whole revival. But to Daniel, only his mission was important. He was there to preach, to win the lost, to see Christians return to their first love. I remembered that fondly, my first love. I was too embarrassed to tell Daniel how on fire I had been over my conversion several years before. I couldn't tell about how I told my mother and then my best friend, and then led him to the Lord. I couldn't tell him how I wanted to do nothing but praise Jesus and tell others about Him.

It was as if that was from a former life. I had lost my first love a long time ago. I began to question my salvation. I died a thousand deaths on that platform, having to give an announcement or two and then introduce Daniel. I was mortified, and it showed. I stumbled, mumbled, stuttered, and muttered, dry-mouthed, till I thought all those so-called friends of mine were going to die trying to keep from cracking up.

I looked at the floor, pawed at the carpet with my shoe, and decided I would never get myself roped into such a thing again as long as I lived. I don't know how I ever thought I was going to be a lawyer. I even got "encouragement" from elders in the church who said kind things like, "We don't all have the same gifts. Don't feel bad that yours is not in public speaking or platform work."

Even the embarrassment of having to sit on the platform every night didn't keep me from coming under conviction when I heard Daniel preach. I fell so short of God's ideal. Daniel quoted Scripture so frequently and easily, naturally dropping it into his exciting sermons, that I knew I should get back into the Word.

Praying through my problem and spending time in the Bible memorizing verses, I came to the realization that I was indeed a Christian; I was just rusty. I had given my life to God, Christ had saved me, but I had drifted far, so far. Those verses started working on my heart, and as I sat there, night after night, God was speaking to me, drawing me closer and closer to Himself. I found I was able to pray for the lost, and to pray that other Christians would have the same experience I was having.

My platform work got no better, and by the last Friday night of the revival, I was glad it was about to end for that reason alone. I did feel closer to Christ. I was committed to staying close and keeping in the Word every day. But I was overjoyed that my responsibilities for the revival were almost over.

That night, after introducing Daniel, I felt God dealing with me. For some reason, despite all my growth during the week and the fact that my duties had ended, I was not relieved. I had no peace. I had some private commitments, and I knew I would be better for Betty and for the church. But God was still dealing with me. I had received assurance about salvation, and I began to pray silently, confessing all known sin. I reaffirmed to the Lord that I meant business about my new dedication to Him, but still my heart was troubled.

I pleaded with God for relief, for Him to indicate to me what He wanted. When I got the first inkling that the Spirit was trying to impress upon me that I should become an evangelist, I discounted it as impossible for two very obvious reasons. First, how would I live? I didn't want to live hand-to-mouth like my mother had. That showed me there was at least one area of my life I hadn't surrendered. But the other reason was even more obvious. "Lord," I prayed, "You know I can't speak in public! I couldn't even give a report in school. How could I preach?"

Then the thing I dreaded most happened. God spoke clearly to my heart. No question this time, no simple impression. This was the real thing. "James, I want you to be an evangelist."

Daniel had finished preaching. People were streaming forward. Daddy Hale stood at the front, welcoming sinners, saved and rededicated. I fought with the Lord. "How can I preach?"

His response was just as clear. "Where is your faith?"

It was so simple, so profound. I wouldn't want to preach on my own power anyway. God's admonition, "Where is your faith?" was all I needed. Though I couldn't imagine myself actually preaching, God was promising that if I had the faith to trust in Him, He would give me the power and the words and even the opportunities to preach for Him.

Betty must have wondered when I stepped out. Mama Hale must have wondered, too. No doubt most folks there knew I had received Christ in that very sanctuary a few years ago, but they also knew I was a boy not close to the Lord. They had to think I was being convicted to get right with God.

I floated down that aisle. Human doubt and fear were pushed aside with confidence from the Holy Spirit. I could hardly believe my own words as I rested my cheek on Daddy Hale's shoulder. "God's just called me to be an evangelist, and I want to do it."

Daddy Hale collapsed, and as he fell, he said, "God's called James to preach!" Mama Hale burst into tears and ran down to be with me. People were crying all over the place. Many sensed the presence of God in that place and knew it was real, crazy as it sounded.

Others could not be convinced. They could not believe God

could use such a shy boy. I later asked a deacon, "Do you think God can use me?"

He tried to evade the question, but my gaze burned into him. He smiled kindly and condescendingly. "Honestly, son, no. Not to preach."

But I knew God had called me. Beyond a shadow of a doubt, I fell so in love with Jesus that my heart overflowed. From that moment I had courage and compassion and zeal without measure. I didn't even have anywhere to preach, but I was ready. I was willing. And because of God alone, I was able.

My friends couldn't believe the change in my personality. Neither could I. Neither could Betty. Some joked that God was calling someone else, and I had overheard the call. But I knew better. I could identify with those who describe the Holy Spirit coming upon them as waves of liquid love pouring into their beings.

That night Daniel Vestal pointed at me and said to the congregation, "This one decision is worth my whole life and ministry."

I was in love with God and with everybody. I could see great masses of lost people, all needing Jesus. I loved them with His love, and I wanted to tell them. I couldn't wait to get started.

I had no idea my first opportunity would come the following Monday.

CHAPTER 8

An Unlikely Start

Saturday and Sunday after my calling to preach, were special days. I went to Sunday school and worship service with a different attitude from any I'd ever had. I wanted to learn all there was to learn, to sing with all my heart, to worship God with my brothers and sisters in Christ. I exulted in my newfound love of Christ, and my friends were amazed. People I wouldn't even look at before might hear me say, "Isn't God good? Aren't we blessed to be able to worship Him today?"

At first I didn't look forward to my job Monday morning. The thought of having to spend time with a bunch of hard-living, bad-mouthing men all day in the hot sun was depressing. But when I thought of all those men and their lost condition, God filled my heart with compassion and pity for them. I prayed I might have an opportunity to lead one to Christ. I prayed for them on the way to PetroTex.

The sun rose high and harsh, alone in a cloudless sky. When the workday started, it was already blistering. The language I had become calloused to would be in full force today. The men swaggered, bragged of sexual conquests, swore, spoke dirty about their wives and mistresses, trying to pass the sweltering morning with macho talk.

It had rolled off my back before. I wasn't one to talk that way. I knew better than that. But I had never called anyone on it. I had laughed at the dirty jokes and maybe shared a few with my friends, but I was too shy to repeat them on the job. I hung back, silent, listening, taking it all in.

That Monday I heard my Savior's name taken in vain so many times that I could hardly stand it; it was breaking my heart. When the two flatbed trucks were moved into position for lunchtime, I was relieved. Finally, a break. Something to drink. A couple of hundred of us would mill about the trucks, some putting their lunch boxes up on the trailers. Some would sit on the ground, some on the trucks. Most would just lean against them, talking, eating, resting, trying to regroup for what appeared to be the hottest August afternoon we could remember.

I sat Indian-style on the ground, my lunch box before me. I bowed my head, not even considering embarrassment. I silently thanked the Lord for my food and for the opportunity to love Him one more day. The sun had sapped the strength from my body, just as it had everyone else's. But my mind and heart were racing. How do you go about winning lost people to Christ? Must I have a seminary degree first? Must I be thoroughly conversant with all Scripture? Must I have a church?

Those men were lost souls. Few of them went to church, and few ever would. I ate slowly, unenthusiastically, my mind in turmoil. I loved Jesus so much that He was loving the men through me. Yet their language, their humor, and their attitudes reviled me. I didn't have time to plan a course of action. If I'd thought about it, I probably wouldn't have done it. I certainly didn't do it on my own.

Suddenly, I leaped from the ground and stood atop one of the flatbed trailers. Before I had even said anything, the two hundred or so men fell silent. I had jumped up to address them all, and somehow they knew it. The last remnants of conversation and laughter died out when I began to speak.

"Listen!" Men stared with whole sandwiches crammed in their cheeks. The shy, nearly unknown laborer in Levis and a T-shirt was standing on the truck, calling for attention. He got it. "Listen to me!" I could hardly believe my own ears! I had never voluntarily addressed any group, least of all a hostile one.

"I'm just a boy out here trying to learn how to be a man!" No one moved, let alone spoke. "All you men are teaching me how to talk filthy, think filthy, live filthy, be filthy!" As the words tumbled out, I felt a boldness come over me, a sense of clarity of mind. I wasn't worrying about what people must be thinking of me. I was preaching! I had been called to preach, and I wouldn't wait any longer.

"Men," I continued, "I wouldn't talk about a dog the way most of you talk about your wives!" I had gotten their attention. I had clarified their problem. But now what? They could have attacked me, killed me, buried me and been done with it. But that same burden for their souls, that heavenly love for the lost, overwhelmed me, gave me the transition I needed. My eyes filled with tears, and I wept as I continued.

"But God loves you! And He gave Jesus to die for you!" I didn't have Scripture references; I didn't have a Bible; I didn't have theological training or biblical languages or anything. I didn't even give an invitation and wouldn't have known how, but still God came upon that place. The Holy Spirit swept over those men. Craftsmen, engineers, pipefitters, insulators, and craftsman's helpers like me sat their stunned.

When I finished no one spoke. I hopped down and gathered my stuff, preparing to go back to work. Men stared at the ground, and soon they shuffled back to their jobs. The place was deathly quiet until one man caught up with me, tears in his eyes. "Help me. I'm just what you said I was."

That was all it took to get things going. Suddenly the bashful, gangly boy who couldn't look anyone in the eye, let alone say hi, was kneeling on catwalks, behind heavy equipment, anywhere handy to lead a man to Christ, to pray for his problem with alcohol or his bad marriage. Little did I realize my evangelistic ministry, which would ultimately touch the world, had begun on a flatbed truck at a construction job.

Daddy Hale had some contacts at East Texas Baptist College in Marshall, on the Louisiana border across from Shreveport. Betty's brother, Pete Freeman, attended there, and with people pulling whatever strings they could, I was accepted for the fall semester. For the next few weeks, while I was preparing for school by earning what money I could at my job, I witnessed to the men, leading them to Christ and praying for them.

The supervisors, the foremen, all knew what was going on, but I never got in trouble. I would work a few minutes, and then someone would ask me to talk with him. It might expand to a half-hour as men twice my age would tell me their problems, ask for prayer, learn how to know Jesus, and kneel and pray with me.

I got so busy with the men that I didn't have time to work. It was as if I was the full-time, paid chaplain of the place. The bosses didn't seem to mind; but some of them came to me, too. In that small, miraculous way, my first ministry was born in the fervor and the power of the Holy Spirit.

I prayed, hard, long, and often about the chance God had given me to attend East Texas Baptist College. It was an opportunity I could hardly believe, and I was determined to make the best of it. I had never been a great student, but I wanted to learn Scripture and theology so badly I could hardly wait to get started. God had given me such a love and a thirst for Him and His Word that I also looked forward simply to getting some private time to commune with Him.

My relationship with Betty changed, too. I think now that she didn't quite know what to make of the new me. She was in love with me. My love for her frankly paled in comparison with my love for God. And for a person with a low self-image— which we both had—it can be difficult to realize that you must compete with God Himself for the love of your life.

All I wanted to do was go to church and Sunday school and whatever revival meetings or evangelistic crusades I could find. If Betty was not as enthusiastic about them at that time, I hardly noticed. I was in my own spiritual world, in love with the things of God. I liked Betty a lot, thought I might be in love with her, but I had higher priorities just then. I wasn't thinking about marriage. I was thinking about college, about preparing to serve God with all my being.

The day I was to leave for college, Hurricane Carla slammed Texas with winds over a hundred miles an hour. I didn't want to miss the first day of school, so I insisted on driving off anyway. "I'll drive real slow," I told the Hales, "but I have to go." As soon as I got onto the highway, I had second thoughts. The car was blown sideways all the way across the freeway, sliding without turning. "Lord, " I pleaded, "You're going to have to take care of me."

I prayed the whole way and finally made it. The registration and initiation process was like another hurricane. The shy boy who loved Jesus was inundated with procedures and formalities, but somehow I got through it. I had the boldness to preach, but I was still deficient in the social graces. I didn't really know how to meet people, and I felt awkward.

In a strange way, that was all right. My retreat from people and from painful situations was to run to God. I spent time with

Him. I wasn't Mr. Personality, but there were already enough Joe College types around. I had come to East Texas Baptist College to fellowship with God.

I enjoyed the classes, but whenever I had a break, I read my Bible. The Word burned in my heart. I had put off serious Bible study for long enough in my life. Now everything seemed new and fresh and real and deep to me. I hungered and thirsted after righteousness. I drank it in, feasted on it, couldn't get enough of it. If I had a fifteen-minute break, I would run across campus and bound up three flights of stairs to my dorm room and fall to my knees. I spent most of my time in prayer expressing my deep love of Jesus and my gratitude to Him for dying for my sins and for loving me.

I witnessed to people on the streets of the town, to other students, to anyone I ran across. The most popular guy on campus, a cheerleader and Baptist Student Union choir director, named Billy Foote, took a liking to me. I could hardly believe it because we were so opposite. But he told me, "James, you're different. It's clear you really love Jesus and care about telling other people about Him."

I asked if he would pray with me sometime, and he said sure. We set a date for after midnight one night, a week later, in the dorm, and until that day came, I thought about it often. Billy Foote was actually going to pray with me.

I explored the countryside around the college until I found a beautiful pine woods, where I would retreat just to walk and talk with God. I told Jesus how much I loved Him and wanted to serve Him. I thanked Him for calling me to preach and for giving me a boldness that was not only above and beyond what I could have mustered, but also went against my very grain of shyness. I knew that it was a miracle and that I could tap it to do whatever He called me to do.

I went to the woods nearly every day, eager to tell the Lord how much I loved Him. His presence saturated the atmosphere, and He seemed to say, "I've been waiting for you. I love you so much, James."

I felt as if I could reach up and take Him by the hand and walk with Him. I'd say, "Jesus, I want to tell people how wonderful You are. I want to tell them how great You are. I want everybody to hear, Lord."

One day He stunned me. He seemed to respond to my expressions of a desire to share His love by telling me that He was going to use me. It was as if He said, "James, I'm going to use you to preach My Word to the world."

I prayed, "God, I can't even think in those terms. I just want to tell others about You."

"Within a year, you will be preaching in the largest churches in America."

"But I've never preached in a church. I'm just a teenager, eighteen years old—"

"And you'll preach in football stadiums and coliseums all over America."

"Lord, I've never preached anywhere but for a minute off the back of a flatbed truck!"

"James, this will happen. I'm going to use you."

As I dropped to my knees in prayer, telling God that He didn't have to give me a big ministry like that, He gave me a glimpse of what it was going to be like. In my mind's eye He inserted pictures of huge churches, stadiums, coliseums filled with people. At the end of my messages, thousands streamed forward to receive Christ.

I was so overwhelmed I could hardly take it in. "Jesus," I said, "all I want it to be is just You and me, right here. No matter what happens, if You give me a big ministry or a small one, I promise I'll always come right back here to You and tell You I love You and wait upon You."

I could imagine Him responding by putting His hand on my shoulder and smiling. I was thrilled with and puzzled by what He had told and shown me, and I was eager to share it with someone. But who would understand? Who wouldn't think that I was a country boy gone mad?

That night as I lay in bed, pondering it all, I looked forward to my prayer appointment with Billy Foote. He was always out having fun, entertaining someone, singing somewhere, or directing the choir. What a thrill to think that the most popular guy on campus would have prayer with me!

When he finally returned about 1:00 A.M., he hadn't forgotten. We hurried to the prayer room, eager to get together with God. We read some Scripture and shared together, and I felt the Lord impressing on me that I should share with Billy what He had told me.

I had no idea how he'd react.

C H A P T E R **9**

Beginning the Journey

"Billy," I said, "there's something I want to tell you, but before I do, you have to promise me that you won't tell anyone else and that you won't laugh at me."

"Of course I won't, James."

"Promise?"

"Of course. What is it?"

I told him what God had told me—that I would be preaching in the largest churches in America within a year and that I would speak to crowded stadiums and coliseums. "Do you think I'm crazy?"

Billy stood and walked slowly to where I sat. I didn't know if he was going to leave, call me stupid, or what. He put his hand on my shoulder. "James, I don't think you're crazy. But I do think we should get on our knees and pray that you'll never get in God's way."

We prayed long and fervently that night, pleading with the Lord never to let me lose my first love for Him, to use me in a mighty way, to remind me of my promise to always come back to Him in private, where it was just Him and me, loving each other.

Billy gave me my first public opportunity to share the love of Christ. He asked if I would travel with the BSU choir he directed and give a short testimony before introducing them. "A testimony? What would I say?"

"Just tell how you became a Christian, and make it clear that anyone could do the same. And tell how God has called you to preach. Not all the details, of course, just the boldness He has given you."

I probably prayed more in anticipation of those brief testimonies than any other speaking engagements I've ever had. Man, I mean we went to those meetings prayed up. The congregation would sing, someone would introduce me for a brief word, then I was to introduce Billy and the choir.

I didn't know how to preach; I didn't really have much to say except tell about my salvation and call to preach. But for some reason, every time I shared, the power of God fell on the congregation. More than once, in some little Baptist church in Texas or Louisiana, I would finish my short testimony and prepare to introduce the choir when people would begin to weep and then make their way to the front.

I hadn't given an invitation; I wouldn't have known how yet. I hadn't asked them or instructed them to come forward, but the Spirit of God used what little I said and convicted people of their sin. They were coming to repent.

Billy and I were taken aback. He and the local pastor and I would deal with the people, but we hardly knew what to make of it. I would take some of the credit if I could. I'm not trying to be falsely modest; because of our prayers before the meetings and, I believe, my sincere willingness to be used as a vessel, God moved in a mighty way.

At almost every church, we were invited back, and they wanted me to preach the next time, not just share a testimony. Billy and I talked about it. He felt it was time that I started accepting those invitations. He offered to sing before I preached. "But, Billy," I said, "I don't have any sermons. I've never even preached one."

"Well, you'd better get some," he said.

I scoured the college library for books of sermons by great preachers and books on sermon preparation. Finally, I was preaching. But I was still so shy, I wasn't really cutting loose. Billy noticed. He wanted to know why I didn't gesture and why I didn't raise my voice the way I did in private when I was really excited about something. "I feel like preaching that way," I admitted. "And I know it would be better, but I'm afraid people would laugh at me."

He really Dutch-uncled me, reminding me that the Spirit of God was using me, not the other way around. "I hate to say this, James, but by holding back on the way God wants you to preach, you're quenching the Spirit."

I started speaking with more voice inflection, but still I gripped the edges of those pulpits and hung on. God began to deal with me about using my hands to share His Word. Still I resisted. "I don't know how to do it."

God led me to the mirror in my room and told me to stand there and gesture as I spoke, doing it until it became natural. He was telling me, "I will teach you how." He also prodded me to balance myself the same way I did on the athletic field, to spread my feet to shoulder width and maintain a good bearing. Slowly but surely, I became more comfortable in the pulpit, just being myself.

In one way, of course, I was not myself at all. If it had been me accepting those speaking invitations all over Texas and Louisiana, I would have stood before those people looking down at

71

the floor, shuffling my feet, and mumbling. I was still shy and withdrawn. But when God gave me holy boldness, and taught me to use gestures, balance, and voice inflection, I became a different person in the pulpit. I felt comfortable. I stepped into the pulpit with confidence and righteous indignation over sin. I was forceful about the truths from the Word and emotional over the lost.

When Billy Foote saw how God was blessing me when I let Him have his way, he said, "From now on, you do what God says." Well, I did, and boy, when I just let go and pulled the trigger, God came to those meetings. Everywhere we went, God went, too. We were zealous for souls. We couldn't drive into a service station without witnessing for Jesus.

The first time I visited my home church after having been away at school for a few months, I realized how much I loved Betty. She was so sweet and nice and loving. I knew she was the only person I needed for the rest of my life. I asked her to marry me. I wasn't aware of the private spiritual battle raging within her at that time. All I knew was that we were meant for each other. I wrote to her frequently, and mostly I kept her up-to-date on my ministry and how much I loved Jesus. Love letters to Betty Freeman were mostly love letters to Jesus.

Billy and I dreamed and planned and prayed about our first-ever revival, scheduled with Pastor Bill Baker at the Eastview Baptist Church of Kilgore, Texas. I hinted at it in a letter to Betty, dated January 4, 1962. A four-cent stamp sent it on its way to her home on East Jackson Street in Pasadena.

Dear precious Betty,
    Oh, how I love you and how I miss you! I know that it is God's will for me to be here. I learn so much and grow spiritu-

ally. Billy Foote and I had a wonderful talk and prayer meeting Tues. night. I feel God really has plans for us.

God can make a great soul-winning team out of us if He chooses. We want to serve God with all we have. We want to see people come to know Christ as Savior and friend.

Betty, how did your friends like your ring? I am so happy I gave it to you. I tell everyone up here that I'm engaged. I love you.

If you still have time to read your Bible, read 1 John, then James, and then Romans.

Billy and I have a couple of churches that are considering us for revivals this summer, and we feel more are coming. Praise the Lord. Tell Daddy [Hale] to inform some of the preachers he knows that Billy and I are really on fire for God and want a full summer of revivals. If they would pray about it and feel God could use us, they should let us know.

Love, love, love, love, love, love, forever in Jesus Christ, James Robison

The more I preached and testified, the more invitations I received to do the same. Though I had had a great first semester at East Texas Baptist and started the second semester with a full head of steam, I was impatient. I felt the Lord urging me to get out there and do more. He had given me the burden, the gift, the vision, and the passion for souls. There would be time for school. I had to preach.

What a shock it was to everyone when Billy Foote and I announced that we were dropping out of school. Daddy Hale cried when I told him. "We were so proud of you, James, getting good grades, following the Lord, doing it the right way. Now you're throwing it all away."

"I can go back to school later, Daddy. I *have* to preach."

"You can preach *and* go to school."

"Not for right now, I can't."

Everyone was against Billy and me making the move. Everyone, that is, except the president of the college. Naturally, he wanted to see us. He asked for our side of the story. We both told him we felt led of God to do this. His reaction was simple. "You'd better do what God says."

And we did. Billy sang and I preached in churches all over the South and Southwest, and more invitations came pouring in. We knew we would have to start using some strategy, so we planned eight-day crusades that went Sunday to Sunday. We scheduled nine of them for that summer; we didn't think we could do more than that.

But we could not be depressed, discouraged, fatigued, or even slowed. We were cookin'. God was blessing. Souls were being saved, Christians made right, church memberships increased, and churches and pastors strengthened. There was nothing in the world I'd rather have done. We were in constant fellowship with the Lord, and our faith was not something we practiced only in front of people. We longed for the gas tank to get low so we could pull into a station and tell somebody about Jesus. We would actually get butterflies in our stomachs and our eyes would well with tears in anticipation of telling people that Jesus loved them.

Hundreds and hundreds of invitations to preach piled up. I hardly knew how to handle them. Many were from the same city. A plan began to emerge in our minds to hold citywide crusades where the churches would cooperate, but right then, we only had time to plan for the next meeting.

Meanwhile, Betty was battling her inner turmoil back in Pasadena. She had grown up in the church. It was her life. She was basically a very bashful, shy person, but she felt free to express herself in church. It was like a home away from home. She loved the people, and she enjoyed participating as a youth group leader. She remembers working very hard to be a good person, striving to do her best, never to disappoint, never to hurt anybody. She just wanted to please people, but it was very hard because something was missing from her life. She didn't really know Jesus, even though she was in the church.

Betty and I had dated since we were fifteen years old, so she, above all, was the most affected—the most shocked—that miraculous, glorious night when I had been called to preach. Overnight I became totally unlike the James Robison she knew.

Betty remembers: "On our dates we would go to revival meetings, or we would memorize Scripture. That's all we did. He loved the Lord so much, and I loved James, so I tried to help him. One night on our way to a revival meeting, James turned to me and said happily, 'You know, Betty, Jesus is as real to me as you are sitting next to me.'

"I looked at him and said, 'He's not that real to me. I've known about Him, I've taught about Him, and studied Him all my life. But He's not that real to me.' I didn't know He could be that real to a person. I didn't ever feel worthy enough to be that close to the Lord."

Just before Betty's nineteenth birthday, we went to a Saturday night meeting where a young man gave his testimony. The Lord must have touched Betty's heart during it, because she began to weep and couldn't stop. On our way out to the car, she was still crying.

As we drove home, she wept some more. Finally, I turned to her. "Betty, what is it? What's the matter?"

The Ministry Explosion

"I'm not sure I'm saved," Betty told me. "I don't think I know the Lord."

My first thought was to tell her not to be ridiculous. She and I both knew she was saved; she was the most faithful girl in our church. I wanted to remind her that no one had done more in church work than she had. But the Lord was clearly telling me "keep quiet." I drove to her house and turned off the engine, but before getting out to open her door (I had eventually learned!), I opened my Bible and shared with her the plan of salvation.

I knew she knew it. She had led others to Christ. She had trained people in how to use the plan of salvation in door-to-door witnessing. She had prayed with people in all-night prayer meetings. She was a very religious girl. But if she needed to be saved, she needed to be saved, and that was that.

I didn't ask her to pray the prayer of salvation. I just shared the Scriptures with her so she would be clear on them and know what to do. I learned later that she went into the house still confused about her salvation. Though she had been very familiar with the way to God, those verses jumped out at her as never before. Her eyes had been opened. She stayed up half the night, praying and asking God to show her whether or not she was truly a Christian.

The next morning she went to the church, went to the young people's department where she and her sister, Helen sang special music, and moved on to teach her junior girls class, which she had been teaching three years. She was a member of the choir, and sometimes she sang a solo before the sermon. She had one to sing that day.

She remembers that when she sat back down her heart "was just aching because I was so confused. I loved Jesus, but I wasn't saved. Yet what would people think? Then the Lord began to speak to me. He said, 'You've got to get rid of that pride. There's no room for that. You've got to come to Me for the first time.' When the invitation came, I didn't know there was anybody in the auditorium but me and God.

"I went forward and fell on my knees and asked Jesus to come into my heart for the first time. I went to the pastor, Rev. Hale, and told him, 'I just got saved, right over there.' He said, 'What do you mean you just got saved? You're the best girl in our church.' I said, 'Please stop telling me how good I am. I'm tired of trying to be what I'm not. I just got saved right over there.'"

As a result of that, the Lord used Betty's testimony immediately, and many adults in our church, Memorial Baptist, Pasadena, came to know the Lord.

Meanwhile, the word was spreading that God's hand was upon a teenage preacher. The eight-day crusades Billy and I had waged the previous summer covered several states, resulting in more than a thousand invitations from twenty-seven states.

By the next February, a year to the day after I had preached my first revival, I was invited as a nineteen-year-old to preach at the Shiloh Terrace Baptist Church in Dallas, a mission church of Dr. W. A. Criswell's First Baptist Church of Dallas. The mission church usually had more than a thousand in attendance. For the revival, the crowd overflowed the auditorium, and more than a hundred were saved; hundreds more renewed their commitments.

From that meeting alone, many, many more invitations to speak poured in. One morning in my mailbox I found among the dozens of letters and requests twenty-five separate invitations to speak in the same city. Of course there was no way I could go to all those churches. We asked if they would work together for a citywide crusade in a stadium or auditorium. The next day, fifteen invitations came from another city. The vision God had showed me a year earlier had come to fruition.

I was consumed with Jesus. I would have preached anywhere in any town or community that wanted to hear His story. But if I went to a small church, by the second night the crowds filled the yard, the parking lot, and the street. People often took turns peeking through the windows. It was incredible. The only churches that could hold our crowds were the big ones. Otherwise, we were in civic auditoriums.

Back then I didn't have the time to stop and consider what was happening. I didn't study it, strengthen the strengths and weaken the weaknesses. I just went. I followed the Lord, did what He said, and let Him bring the increase. I knew it was not of my own doing. I was basically an uneducated teenager who was only a year past being too shy to meet people. Now I was as bold as a lion in the pulpit, pacing all over the platform, shouting, whispering, crying, laughing, pointing, gesturing, and preaching my heart out.

All I knew or cared about was doing the will of God. He gave me a message, and I preached it for all I was worth. I'm sure there was some appeal or attraction or at least intrigue in the idea of a kid so young preaching at the top of his lungs. But the bottom line was that God was blessing obedience. He could have taken the best seminary student, the best preacher boy, the one with the best connections, and made him a successful evangelist. But He had called me out of nowhere—drew me to love Him because He first loved me—and had chosen to anoint my life, ministry, message, and delivery.

In February of 1963, Betty and I wanted to get married. My real mother wouldn't hear of it. I had turned nineteen only the previous October, and in Texas at that time, a boy under twenty-one had to have a parent's signature to marry. I tracked down my father in a California prison, and he readily signed. My prayer was that someday I would be more than able to express my gratitude to him by seeing that he would love to know Jesus as Lord and Savior.

Betty and I had thirty dollars to our names after the wedding ceremony, and we had planned a two-day honeymoon in an inexpensive motel in Galveston. Our car, a little Corvair with the engine in the back, was hidden in a garage of the country home of Allen Buchanek, a young man I'd recently led to Christ. One of my ushers, George Cheshire, ran us out there to elude anyone trying to follow us.

In spite of the light rain that was falling, we happily threw all our stuff into the little car and raced off toward Galveston. But wait, was that someone in our rearview mirror, trying to follow us? I thought I better not take any chances. I sped up and was going over fifty around a tight curve, one I could have handled on a dry day. The Corvair went into a spin, and the rear engine whipped us around three times like a child's toy top.

We spun across the oncoming lane of traffic, narrowly missing a car, then wound up in the ditch on the other side of the road, just missing a telephone pole. Betty's overnight case, which had been on the back window shelf, had flown into the front seat with us. Our knees were like jelly, and we knew God had miraculously spared us. We could have been killed or terribly injured, but I was able to pull the car back onto the road. After we prayed, thanking God we were still alive, I drove much more carefully the rest of the way, and we decided that no one had been following us in the first place.

I got our room key and lugged our stuff up the stairs and into the room, only to discover there was no bed. We hadn't asked for the honeymoon suite, but for cryin' out loud. . . . I called the front desk. "Hey, where's the bed up here?"

I was informed that we were in a studio room.

"I don't care what you call it. We got to have a bed, man!"

He told me it was under a cabinet by the wall. Our first adventure was finding the thing and pulling it out. It was made up of two single beds that rolled out and fit together. We flopped down onto it to see how it worked and realized that it would be all we could do to keep the two sections from rolling apart. It wasn't such a hot deal, but the price was right.

I got ready for bed, and Betty went into the bathroom to get ready. She finally came out in her beautiful new gown, and we were happy to be there together, starting our lifetime of marriage. Suddenly we heard a key in the lock. It was jiggling. I tensed. The key was working! The knob was turning, the latch was loosening, the door was opening. . . .

I sprang from the bed and kicked the door while in the air, catching the intruder in midstride and sending him flying back to the railing at the top of the stairs. I'm surprised I didn't kill him. I yelled, "Hey, there's somebody in here!"

"Oh, we're sorry" came the weak and shocked reply. "They gave us the key."

"Well, it's the wrong room," I said sharply. Then I was on the phone again. "Hey, first it's no bed, and now you send somebody else to our room! We just got married and this is *our* room! Quit giving people the key!"

We wound up bolting the door, chain-locking it, and jamming a few pieces of furniture up against it for good measure. Of course, the furniture in a place of that quality wouldn't have protected us from much, but we felt more secure.

We didn't have a big agenda for our honeymoon. We spent most of the time strolling the sandy beach and dining on fried shrimp. We still laugh at an old movie Betty shot of me coming out of the office of that motel after paying the bill two days later. I held up the only two dollars we had left.

I loved Betty so much that I was stunned years later to discover that she suffered from severe doubts about her worthiness to be my wife. No such thought ever entered my head because she was so petite and pretty and sweet. I couldn't have asked for anything more.

But she remembers that Satan was filling her head full of lies about herself: "When I went to James's services, I never wanted to sit up front where I'd be noticed. I was too intimidated. I pleaded with him not to introduce me. And when I sat in the crowd, Satan would point out certain women to me and force me to compare myself to them. He'd say, 'You see that lady over there? Look how pretty she is. That's the kind of wife he needs. She's so striking. She's got it all together.' Then I might meet her and discover that she indeed had many gifts. She could teach; she had a tone of authority; she carried herself with confidence. I felt I had none of those things, and my heart would be crushed.

"Satan didn't stop there. He convinced me that I would die young so that James would be able to find the right woman for him, the right mother for his children. I was scared I would die from something terrible like cancer, the way my father did. I accepted that lie as truth and began to die inside. I suspected every symptom and was so convinced that my next physical would show cancer everywhere, I lived in misery all the time."

How I wish I had known all that back then! I loved Betty so deeply that I believe I could have helped build her confidence. But it was her secret, and I wouldn't learn it until years later. By then it was almost too late for me to do anything to help her, not just because her feelings of inferiority were so ingrained, but also because I had severe problems of my own by then.

I enrolled in San Jacinto Junior College soon after we got married, and the basketball coach there encouraged me to try out for the team. He was a Christian and had played against me in the church league. He knew I had led the league in scoring with a 25-point average and averaged 48 points in the college intramural program, so he wanted me to try out head-to-head with their all-state and all-American guard. He really thought I had a chance against his star player.

We went at it, one-on-one, and somehow, I beat the socks off him. I could leap and shoot, and he simply couldn't stay with me. The coach offered me a full scholarship, trying to talk me into coming for two years on a free ride. "Can't do it," I told him. "I get out preachin', and I'm liable not to come back for a few weeks. Could miss a lot of games that way."

He was sympathetic. He knew me. Knew I would put preaching ahead of basketball. And he also knew my priorities were right. As it turned out, they didn't need me, but it sure would have been fun. San Jacinto won the national junior college championship that next season.

Another reason I simply couldn't have accepted the scholarship was that I had promised myself and a few others, the Lord included, that I would return to East Texas Baptist for more Bible training. But before that, during the summer between my semester at San Jacinto and the new term at East Texas, I would see a revival in my old high school unlike anything the city of Pasadena had ever seen.

Breakthrough at Pasadena High

Having been a sports fan throughout high school, I knew all the Pasadena High school stars and followed the games. I was better at basketball, but probably because I had been restricted somewhat from football, it fascinated me most.

I had tried to witness to several of the players, and they were shocked. They remembered me from when I was a senior, a quiet, shy, tall kid with nothing to say. I wasn't a troublemaker or anything, but they hadn't seen me as part of any religious crowd. They heard I was an evangelist drawing big crowds, and like everyone else, they could hardly believe it.

When I was booked for a week of meetings in August at a local church, Southmore Plaza Baptist, a few of the players came out just to see what was going on. How we prayed for those boys! We knew that if God could save a few of them, the team and the school would be tremendously affected. The key guys were all-state quarterback Ricky Carlisle, running back Frank Hale (one of the toughest guys on the team), and split end

George Cheshire, a junior who was second only to Frank as the toughest player. (George would prove to be the toughest the next year, and he was also the most popular student that year, voted Mr. Pasadena High School.)

The word was that Frank Hale might be a Christian, so we weren't terribly surprised when he showed up at the meetings the first night. We were hoping he'd get right with God and either distance himself from the bad influence of the rest of the big jocks or witness to them. They were a tough crowd, most popular on campus, had all the best-looking girls, and were big drinkers and carousers. It wasn't going to be easy to talk them out of what they considered the most fun in their lives, but Jesus wanted them for Himself.

Sure enough, Frank Hale came forward that night and asked to talk with me. The Lord had been dealing with him, and he was ready to live for God all the time. I rejoiced and counseled and prayed with him. He really meant business. With tears in his eyes, he vowed, "James, if you'll help me, I want to get the whole football team out here sometime this week."

"The whole team?"

"All of 'em! Why not?"

He made the rounds of the pool halls and other hot spots in town late one afternoon, and Frank and a few of his buddies put the arm on their friends, inviting some, challenging others, until a huge bunch of Pasadena High football players promised to come to the meeting. There must have been forty of them, but the hotshot junior, George Cheshire, didn't want to join them.

"Man, I'd rather go to Galveston tonight," he told Frank and his friends. "Think of a trunkload of iced-down beer and the ladies we'll meet. Come on!"

Frank and two other seniors pulled him aside. In a few minutes they all came back. George looked a little sheepish. "I'll come," he said, "but I'm coming in style. Then I'm on my way to

Galveston to get drunk and have some fun, and anybody who wants to join me can. . . . I'll bet almost everyone will."

I asked Frank how they had persuaded him to come. "We just told him what we'd do to him if he didn't show up." (Well, there are all kinds of methods of evangelism!) Jesus said, "Compel them to come in, that my house may be filled" (Lk 14:23). I guess Frank took him seriously.

In those days, in the fire of the Spirit, I was always inspired to preach. But when forty-some football players from the local high school, not to mention cheerleaders and many others, helped pack a church, man, I was ready. We were prayed up. We wanted to see God change those kids, that school, that town. Just a few of us really believed it could happen.

George showed up with his car sagging in back and water dripping steadily from the ice in his trunk. As I sat on the platform during the song service, I saw him saunter in the back and plant himself right behind a row of pretty girls. During the service, he tapped them on the shoulders, whispered in their ears, told them jokes, and generally made a nuisance of himself to them and everyone else around them. I was getting steamed, but I just kept praying for him.

During the singing, he made fun of the songs, singing falsetto, then off key, then as loud as he could. He was a funny guy, and some of the kids around him couldn't help laughing. I stared at him, but he carefully avoided my gaze.

When I finally got up to preach, ol' George slouched back in the pew and put his feet on the back of the pew in front of him. He started picking fuzz balls off the woolen socks he had stolen from the high school athletic department. He rolled a couple of fuzz balls and laid them in his palm, then blew on them until they floated high into the air, dancing over people's heads and then resting in hairdos or on shoulders. Of course this caused snickers all around, and George went at it in earnest. People from several rows around him watched the show, while I tried to preach.

I could see those fuzz balls darting around and floating onto people, too, and I was angry. In the flesh I could have easily called him down, shouted at him, been sarcastic, and run him off. Normally, I might have. I consider it the height of blasphemy to distract people from hearing the preaching of the Word of God, but something told me just to keep going, keep preaching Jesus.

I spoke louder, used wider gestures, and preached my heart out. For more than fifteen minutes, I competed with George Cheshire's fuzz ball show. Finally, I preached right at him. He still avoided my gaze, but I intended to break through. I don't remember where I was in my sermon or what I said, but suddenly, he lowered his feet, sat up, leaned forward, put his elbows on his knees and his chin in his hands, and stared right back at me. I felt it when he felt it. The power of God fell on that boy. He was getting it full in the face—actually, deep down in his heart.

Of course, when God is in a place, He doesn't just rest on one person. The sanctuary was permeated with the presence and the power of God. Everyone could feel it. All was eerily silent except for the boom of my voice. No one moved. No one even fanned his face, in spite of the heat.

When I gave the invitation to those who wanted to receive Christ, George came roaring out of that pew. He pushed people aside and rushed down the aisle, the first to arrive. He dropped to his knees at the altar, and as I invited more to come and gave instructions to those who had come, suddenly George headed for the pulpit.

In midsentence, I was stiff-armed aside. He grabbed the microphone. "Excuse me, brother," he said. "I want to say something." He then raised his voice to the audience composed of many of his schoolmates and teammates. "Listen, I came here tonight to wreck this meeting. My trunk is full of iced-down beer, and I was gonna get all my teammates to go to Galveston with me and get drunk. Instead, the greatest thing ever in my life just happened. I got Jesus. I'm saved!"

When he sat down, that place fell apart. People who had been Christians for years wept and got right with God. A total of twenty-eight Pasadena High School football players streamed down the aisle and got saved. Several other high-school boys and girls came forward. Kids today talk about something being awesome. Man, that was awesome! And it wasn't just some emotional deal that wore off. George Chesire became a zealot for Christ. They all did. That team would meet for prayer before the game. After every game they invited the opposing team to kneel with them at the fifty-yard line to thank God that no one was seriously hurt and to lead others to Christ.

During one game, the other team was about to kick off in the fourth quarter with the score tied, and no one could find Cheshire, the Pasadena return man. Finally, someone noticed him kneeling in prayer at the end of the bench. He scampered onto the field just in time to field the kick and run it all the way back for a touchdown and the victory. They had a fabulous year, too, going all the way to the district championship before losing 0–6 on a ninety-yard pass interception. They had outgained their opponents three hundred yards to sixty and made twenty-four first downs to six.

Ricky Carlisle, Mr. Pasadena High School, and his date, the head cheerleader, who had been named prom queen, broke tradition that year and anounced that they weren't going to the prom. School officials threatened to take away all their honors, but Ricky and his date didn't care. All the Christians boycotted the prom, and when the other students got wind of the threats from the officials, they didn't go either. It was the lowest prom attendance the school ever had, and the next year—when George Cheshire was Mr. Pasadena High School—the result was the same. That year, the football team went all the way to the state quarter finals before losing a tie game on penetrations.

From there, our ministry was off and running. I went back to East Texas Baptist College and tried to finish, but by then our beautiful daughter, Rhonda, had been born and we were on the move. Rev. T. D. Hall, a Dallas area pastor, invited me to preach in his church, and we started a lifelong friendship that saw him working with our ministry for many years. We traveled all over the United States, speaking in the large churches and holding citywide crusades. I made it into my senior year, and I learned a lot, but I never finished.

I was preaching in a local high-school stadium one night when Dr. W. A. Criswell came to hear me. He had, of course, been aware of our meetings at Shiloh Terrace, his mission church, so he wanted to see what we were about. By the time I was twenty-two, he had asked me to come preach in his church, First Baptist, Dallas, any time I wasn't on the road. That wasn't very often, but what a privilege! I took him up on it, and that opened even more doors for us.

Betty knew I would never get the sports bug out of my system. We still laugh over the fact that on our wedding day I played in a state church play-off basketball game. I scored 22 points in the first half, all on long field goals, and shot 100 percent. I never had a half like that, before or since. In the second half my defender played me man-to-man from the time I brought the ball up until just across midcourt, where two teammates joined him. Triple-teamed, I was unable to shoot again. All I could do was pass, but with two others on my team left in the open, we won.

At East Texas Baptist, I immersed myself totally in intramurals whenever I was in town. I was awarded the Most Valuable

Player trophies in both basketball and football, averaging nearly 50 points a game in basketball with the ability to dunk before it was that popular.

In football, our team was undefeated, untied, and unscored against. I played on both offense and defense, and I was a fighter. People came just to see what ol' Robison would do. On offense I played quarterback until we got into trouble, then I would play end and go out for a pass. I'd say, "Just throw it up. I'll get it." I was taller than most and could jump so high that somehow I just got to the ball.

I confess there were times when I was angry with God for having put me in a situation with a mother who wouldn't let me participate in sports. I loved it so much and I obviously had ability, yet I wasn't able to play competitively until it was too late. My interest in sports became an obsession later in my ministry when I couldn't pass a golf course without stopping and trying to break the course record. I broke a few, too. Some months I would consistently shoot in the 60s, and some thought I could have played on the pro tour, but I seriously doubt it. In tennis, I was so dominant and so angry when I didn't do well that no one wanted to play with me. Ministry partners would be embarrassed at what I pulled on the court.

But all that would come out in later years when I was fighting inner battles that threatened to do me in. Back in the early days, when we were at the prime of our lives, young and in love, no one could have convinced Betty or me that we would ever have deep struggles. She was going through the self-doubt that I didn't know about, but she never doubted my spiritual vitality. In truth, the very fact that I seemed to be so devout and victorious made her feel worse. She did not expect me to ever fall.

No one did. Those were the days. Everything we did seemed to result in victory. We had all we wanted and needed. We were not rich, but we weren't striving to be. All I wanted to do was preach, and I was doing enough of that for ten men. We traveled constantly, driving everywhere.

One day when Rhonda was about three, someone asked her where she lived. "I live in the car," she said.

We all did. And we loved it. I was going to keep preaching and obeying God and following Him to whatever crowds He brought my way. I loved Jesus. Betty loved Jesus. Rhonda was brought up in an atmosphere of loving Jesus.

We thought nothing could stop us or even slow us down. Little did I realize that I had allowed the enemy an inroad: I was too busy, too successful for the intimate, personal devotion time with Jesus.

Daddy Joe, My Father

Betty and Rhonda and I were living in a tiny house trailer about ten feet by fifty feet in Pasadena when I got the news that my daddy had been released from jail in California and was heading back to Texas. I didn't know what to think. I couldn't have him in our home with our baby. She was so sweet.

Fortunately, I thought, Daddy Joe settled in a cheap boarding house a few miles away. Once, when I hadn't seen him around for a few days, I went to the boarding house to find him. The place smelled horrible, and as a young, decently dressed preacher, I know I looked out of place. The transients stared as I found my way to his room.

I was heartbroken just to see the squalor. I had grown up in poverty, but not in a rancid stench like that. Daddy's door was open a few inches. I pushed it farther and found him lying there in his own vomit. He was in such a stupor he couldn't even open his eyes. I knelt and held him in my arms, the combination of body odor, cheap wine, and vomit sickening me.

In the flesh, I should have hated him, but God had given me such a burden for his soul that I couldn't do anything but pray for him. He lay there awkwardly in my arms, and I rocked him, weeping till my tears rolled over him and onto the floor. He was in and out of consciousness, and I sobbed, "Daddy, I don't even know you, but I love you. I want you to be saved."

He shook his head. "Son, I just can't be. I just can't."

"Yes, you can."

I helped him get cleaned up and pleaded with him to go to Freddie Gage's Pulpit in the Shadows ministry, a halfway house for drug addicts and alcoholics. They tried to help him, and all the while I was urging him to go with me to Daddy Hale's church. Finally, he agreed.

That morning during the invitation, I went forward with him, hoping and praying for the best. Surely he meant it and would truly believe. I helped him pray the sinner's prayer, but I wasn't as happy as I should have been. I knew that something wasn't right.

"Well, Daddy, now you should be baptized."

"No!" he shouted. "No more! I won't do any more!"

"Well, you need to be part of a church family."

"No, I don't want anything to do with that."

Clearly, something was wrong. He had obviously gone forward just to please me, though he had said he really wanted to be saved.

Before the week was out, I was driving home one day when I saw a man lying in the gutter, his face turned toward the drain. He wasn't moving. I pulled over and hurried across the street to help him, wondering if he was alive. I gently took his shoulder and slowly rolled him onto his back. Suddenly, I found myself looking into the face of my own father. I was shocked.

"Daddy!"

"Son, I'm sick," he managed. "I'm so sick."

Of course, he was drunk, and I couldn't let him go back to the boarding house, but I couldn't let him inside our trailer either. He had nearly killed my mother while he was in a drunken stupor, and he had threatened to do the same to me. I couldn't risk the lives of my wife and daughter, so I let him sit outside in a lawn chair for two days while he sobered up. He slept most of the time, and before we knew it, he was off on his own again. Soon, he was back in jail.

Not long afterward, I was preaching a series of meetings in Lockhart, Texas, near Austin, when I heard that my daddy was in the Austin area. I asked around until I located him. He looked terrible, older than his age, worse than ever. "Daddy," I said, "I'm preachin' not far from here, and we're having a great time. The stands are full every night, and the Lord is blessing all of us. People are getting saved. I wish you would hear me preach just once."

He looked away and spoke softly. "I wouldn't have a way to get there."

"I'd come and get you. I'd pick you up at six, and you'd be my guest."

"I've got nothin' decent to wear."

"That's all right. It's outside at a stadium. You can wear whatever you want. Nobody will bother you. You'll really enjoy it."

I wanted him to come so badly. First, I wanted him to be saved. Then I just wanted him to see me, to hear me, just once. I knew I was nothing, a nobody from nowhere. I didn't want to brag, but it was clear that God was in my life, that I had been led to serve Him by preaching to the masses. I hoped my daddy would be proud to see what his son had become.

He spoke so softly I could hardly hear him. And he still wasn't looking at me. "I guess that'll be all right."

"Huh?"

"That'd be okay. If you come get me, I'll go."

"You mean it?"

"Sure."

"Great. I'll see you at six!"

I was overjoyed, and I prayed for him the rest of the afternoon as I prepared for the evening's message. When I returned at six to pick him up, he was obstinate. Not ugly, just firm. "I can't go, son. I just can't go."

"Why not, Daddy?"

"I just can't."

I pleaded with him, reminding him that he had promised, telling him how nonthreatening it would be, how easy we would make it for him. He wouldn't budge. I tried to hide my bitter disappointment, and I simply told him good-by as I left.

A couple of weeks later I was preaching a mid-cities crusade between Dallas and Fort Worth, when a call came. The folks at a funeral parlor in Round Rock, north of Austin, informed me of my father's death and asked if they should expect me at his funeral the next day. I told them of course, and hung up, expecting to weep. But I seemed unable. How I wish he'd gone with me that night!

John McKay was the crusade singer at that time, and he agreed to drive Betty and me to Round Rock. When we got there the next afternoon my mother and my aunt had arranged a small service to be led by a local pastor. They delayed the beginning of the funeral because none of the pallbearers—four of Daddy's drinking buddies—had arrived. They never showed. The world's crowd never provides real friends.

Finally the funeral home director informed my mother that he had secured the services of four men who had agreed to serve as honorary pallbearers. I could tell by the way they looked that one of them might have been a helper at the parlor and the other three had been found on the street and offered a few dollars.

The local pastor, my mother, my aunt, the four "pallbearers,"

Betty, John McKay, and I were the only people at the funeral of a man who had lived sixty-three years. It was so sad. Kindly, John agreed to sing.

As I stood by that coffin, looking into the chalky face of a man dressed more neatly than I had ever seen him, I felt as if I should cry. But I couldn't. I know I seemed hardhearted. I prayed to be able to cry, but the Lord spoke to me: "You did your crying before he died. You did all you could."

I hadn't waited to cry until he died. I had wept over him. I tried to help him. I walked down the aisle with him. I tried to win him. God had given me a love for a man who never once expressed love to me, who had never bought me a pair of shoes or socks or a bite to eat in his life. He had stolen my savings when I was a young teen, and yet I loved him.

I know when I get to heaven I'll be in for a lot of surprises, but there's none I want more than to see a hand wave out of a crowd on a street of gold and to hear a voice I recognize say, "Look here, son, it's your dad." I want to hear him say that after I left him that last time and drove off, he went to bed and when his head hit the pillow, he prayed, "Lord, be merciful to me a sinner." I want him to tell me that God saved him.

Maybe it never happened. I know it's not likely. But I do know one thing with absolute certainty: I worship a God with that kind of love and grace.

C H A P T E R **13**

Hard Lessons

A couple of years ago, God reminded me of the good old days in ministry, and He did it in a gentle, unusual way that really drove home the point. The pilot of our ministry's Falcon jet was cruising along between five and six hundred miles an hour when a young preacher traveling with us said, "James, God sure has blessed you to give you this airplane."

I nodded absently and said, "Yes, He sure has. Praise the Lord." The ministry had owned its own planes since 1968 when I began piloting myself around to stay on schedule. But as we streaked over east Texas, God dealt with me. Whether anyone else said anything to me, I couldn't say. All I know is, in my mind and heart, I had a running conversation with the Lord. He was checking up on me.

"James, do you think I died to give you a jet? I didn't die to give you a jet. Do you think I'm blessing you any more today in this jet than I was when you were down there on those highways, eighteen years old in a worn-out Chevy with all four windows rolled down to keep you from burning up? You barely had enough gas to get to the next town, but when you got near a little gas station, you'd get butterflies in your stomach and tears would well up in your eyes because you knew you were about to get the chance to tell someone how much God loved him and that He died for him.

"Do you think this airplane is why I died? James, I came to give you what you had when you drove that Chevrolet. If you can have that same zeal, that same love, that same joy, and that same compassion sitting here in this airplane, everything is all right."

I sensed the Lord telling me that He wanted me to live an overcoming life, a life that wins, a life that counts.

I have always felt that He sent me talented staff members to accomplish this goal. As Billy Graham had his Wilson brothers—Grady and T. W.—as compatriots, advisers, and friends over the years, I also have had a pair of brothers who have meant the world to me. T. D. and Dudley Hall are men who have ministered with me—but, more important, *to* me—almost since the beginning.

T. D. was pastor of the First Baptist Church of Hurst, Texas, and he became my first crusade director, serving for about nine years. We're still closely associated, involved together in church meetings and various other efforts.

Dudley, his younger brother, was a football player in Alabama who heard me preach at the Falls Creek, Oklahoma, youth camp—the same place my crusade soloist Jeanne Rogers was saved. Dudley was filled with the Spirit, and it changed his whole life. He has been an associate and a teacher at my side, a special counselor and friend.

The Hall brothers were with me when I first encountered what I now see as a satanic attack against me and my ministry. About five years into my crusade work, when the record-breaking attendance numbers were being racked up and everyone seemed to be predicting that I would be the next Billy Graham, I became aware that I carried infection in my blood. I had so many nagging ailments that I couldn't begin to count them.

Beginning back then and continuing ten to fifteen years, I suffered severe, chronic sore throats that hurt me nearly every time I preached. I went to the doctor, if not several crusades in a row, then at least every second or third one. I constantly worried and wondered how I would be able to continue preaching, to get through each night, let alone another week or two of meetings.

I had such bad allergies that I had to take all kinds of antibiotics, but they seemed to have no effect on me. For the last five or six years before I was delivered of my physical ailments, I developed a stomach disorder that left me so nauseated at every third or fourth meal that I nearly passed out.

Everything in my body ached, my glands, my organs, every part of me. My throat, my stomach, my prostate, my kidneys, my sinuses—if I was aware of a bodily function, I had a problem with it. I had backaches something terrible. Every morning I had to go through a painful stretching exercise just to loosen those muscles so I could move about during the day. It was awful.

I accepted sickness as a way of life, but it caused me to live defeated. What a frustration, to be blessed of God with a marvelous ministry, with crowds and reactions and responses no man deserves, and not to be able to enjoy it and be thankful for it because I was in such physical distress! The absolute biggest names in ministry were individually and independently telling me that I was the best preacher they had ever heard. One, whose name is a household word, said I was "the most anointed, the greatest preacher in the world."

I'm thankful that one problem I didn't have was bigheadedness; there was enough praise coming during those early years to bring a man down if he'd let it. No matter what was said or who said it, I knew the truth: God had given me a unique ability to communicate. I knew that especially because it came upon me overnight. I went from being a backward, shy, dirt-kickin', gangly teenager to a man who was able to preach with boldness.

I was humbled by the praise of such men, and I was thankful for their love for me. And I still am. But I was also very much aware that they knew that the glory was due to God, not me. In telling me those kind things, they were giving the glory to God for being so great that He would use somebody like me so effectively. I am overwhelmed by the greatness of God and the fact that other men recognize how great our God is. That is why I do not feel it is a personal compliment to James Robison for his ability when people praise my work.

To be very honest, when men of such stature and anointing and gifts are kind enough to say such things, often it has the opposite effect of puffing me up. Sometimes, it puts me to shame. In so many ways I feel as if I have been a poor steward of the gift God gave me. Many days I'm convinced that I haven't yet touched the surface of what God wants from me. And back in the formative years of the ministry, I came dangerously close to squandering my gift while hardly knowing it.

I knew that Billy Graham was an overt supporter of mine because he once called me on the phone and told me I had preached what he felt was the finest sermon he had ever heard. "You're the greatest gospel preacher in the world," he said. What a thing for a twenty-six-year-old evangelist to hear from the man most people think is truly deserving of that description!

Earlier in my life Billy Graham initiated a visit from Walter Bennett and Fred Dienert of the Walter Bennett Advertising Agency. Walter was Billy's media representative, the one who had initiated the "Hour of Decision" on the radio and put Billy on television for his occasional crusade specials. Back when ABC television was selling other than commercial time, Walter and Fred talked him into purchasing prime time. It had been a major breakthrough for evangelism.

Bennett and Dienert told me that they had been unsuccessful in trying to get Billy to agree to going on the air weekly. They said he told them while on vacation in Mexico that "there's a young preacher I believe has a word from God, and you need to see him, because I believe he's the one who needs to be on television."

According to Fred Dienert, I was that young preacher. "Billy is not interested in a weekly program," he told me. "He says God spoke to him about you."

"Well, I'll pray," I told him, and it cost me five consecutive sleepless nights. During that time, God revealed to me His plans for my television ministry. In a way, it was all a surprise to me because I had been so successful in live meetings. Our crusades were reaching the biggest audiences in the United States. Between the ages of twenty-four and thirty-two, I packed the largest coliseums every eight days, breaking the attendance records everywhere we went. By then, more than ten million people had attended our live crusades in the United States alone.

Yet God wanted me on television, too. It would be expensive, complicated, and not without dangers as well as opportunities, but before I could become completely immersed in it, other things cropped up in my ministry and my personal life. Somewhere between my twenty-sixth and twenty-seventh birthdays, I began to detect differences in my life, and I eventually felt driven to discuss them with T. D. Hall.

By then, T. D. was my crusade director, setting up all the citywide crusades. One day, on our way to watch a football game, I said, "T. D., I can remember when I loved Jesus so much that I couldn't watch a football game without witnessing to people all around the stadium. I remember loving Jesus so much that I couldn't eat in a restaurant without witnessing."

He nodded silently.

"T. D., I remember when I loved Jesus so much that I couldn't do anything with joy, really, except for fellowshiping with God. I remember those days when nothing else in the world meant so much to me."

T. D. began to weep. "James," he said, "I wish it was still that way."

"I know," I said. "You know, I just stay so busy all the time." Something was happening inside me. I detected it, but I didn't know what it was. Hundreds and even thousands were saved in our crusades. God was blessing, even though I had admitted to T. D. that Jesus didn't have first place in my life. Reading my Bible didn't give me the same joy it once had. It was just a tool of the trade, something from which I derived a sermon. The seeds of defeat were being sown in my life.

Something else hit me hard. I listened to so many pastors and preachers criticizing one another that I thought I would scream. I know now that God was preparing me for a message He would give me much later in my ministry, but at the time, all I knew was that I was being dragged down by the constant bickering.

From the time I started going from church to church as a young preacher, I heard criticism of the "other" pastor up the street or across town—all the things he did wrong, why he couldn't be trusted, why he could never cooperate with another certain pastor. Preachers discussed one another and their differences in doctrine until it was clear they had little or no real love, zeal, or willingness to work together.

I felt like a pawn. Too many times I had to be the sole possession of this church or that church or denomination, and all the pastor wanted to talk about was what *his* church was doing. If cooperating with another church would widen the outreach, that was just too bad. Pastor *A* could never do that with Pastor *B* because. . . .

I pushed for taking the name *Baptist* off our crusade literature so that the meetings would welcome people from all denominations in each city. But that only raised tension. Often pastors would say, "This is a meeting *we're* sponsoring, and we're going to put our name on it." It almost seemed that publicizing the name of the church, not cooperating with others to spread the Word of God, was what was important to them.

Then I met some preachers who would say, "Well, the Pentecostals can participate and help sponsor, but they can't counsel or sit on the platform. We don't want anybody on the platform who is not an absolute Bible believer," *Bible believer* meaning anybody who agreed with them right down the line on every point of doctrine, major or minor.

At first I resisted this idea, but eventually, it became part of me. If you didn't agree with me, if you weren't a Southern Baptist or at least a Baptist, a Fundamentalist, you were wrong in your beliefs. Even these groups attacked one another, but still, this became part of my own message. I got a lot of amens from my kind when I said what they really wanted to hear. They wanted to stand out as the only true believers, and I played right into their hands.

I went into churches all over the country, and I found Christians living in defeat, Christians who didn't love God, who had no compassion for the lost or courage to face the world. I became very angry. I thought my anger was righteous indignation against a sleeping church. I began to lash out at the ensnarement of religion (the practice of man trying to reach God) because I detested it. But I didn't realize that it had already permeated my life. Religion had put its tentacles around me. I was into a "form" of preaching, but the love, the compassion, and the brokenness of Christianity (God trying to reach man) were gone.

I had always practiced the biblical admonition not to let the sun go down upon my wrath. If I got out of fellowship with others, I couldn't sleep until I got right with them. But now I found myself going to sleep at night with anger in my heart toward some preacher or even toward some church or city.

Without my knowing it things like religious idolatry, being enamored with religious success, vanity, bitterness, resentment, unforgiveness, judgmentalism, criticism, pride, and self-seeking were creeping into my life. The Word of God was a dull, dead, silent book to me. It was meaningless in my hands.

I still heard from God from time to time. He clearly led me into television. But when that ministry began to multiply, so did all my troubles. What had been a problem on a small scale became a major crisis. God would say to me, "James, you need a message from Me. You're just preaching sermons. You're not saying what I want to say to My people."

Recapturing a Childhood

I'm not proud of what I'm about to relate. It is nothing but sin. Plain and simple, it was wrong. But you'll see how, in my foolishness and shortsightedness and self-centeredness, I justified it.

Part of the problem of my falling into defeat, I know now, was the fact that I felt robbed of a childhood. I was robbed of a father. I was robbed of sports involvement. I was robbed of the things most kids get to do. Something deep inside me was wounded through that, and I didn't realize that I had set about to blame it all on God.

Because I felt robbed, I began to take from God, to take the time and the devotion that belonged to Him. I was an adult in charge of my own ministry, my own life, and my own schedule. I was the boss. I answered to no one but me and a loving board of directors, and I did what *I* wanted. I was still active in ministry, of course, and I still loved God. But who was going to tell me that I couldn't have a little fun in life, that I couldn't play any sport I wanted any time I wanted? No one.

I began to play tennis, and once I caught onto the game, I played six days a week. I had a big, booming serve, and I would run my opponent to death with well-placed shots from near the net. My ministry partners and I played a lot of doubles, and we would take on high-school champs all over the country. We got quite good.

I was a wild man on the court. Jeanne Rogers, my crusade soloist, began to wonder about my relationship with God because of my violent temper. If I missed a shot or lost a match or did something I knew I should have done better, I threw rackets, smashed them, kicked things, shouted, and pouted. My behavior was embarrassing and humiliating to my staff, and it should have been to me, but I was out of control.

Then I began to play golf, and that became a five or six-day-a-week obsession, too. I couldn't pass a golf course, private or public, without yielding to the urge to take a shot at the course record. Within a year after I took up the game, by playing eighteen and sometimes as many as twenty-seven or thirty-six holes a day, I was shooting par. Within another year I consistently shot in the 60s and held three course records. One, a 63, was on a fifty-year-old course and still stood the last time I checked.

If anyone even thought to question my obsession with sports, I defended myself with what seemed to be utter logic. I had a right to do it. I never got to participate in sports as a child. I didn't have a childhood. I was indulging myself because God owed it to me.

I began spending more time planning my daily golf outing than I did planning sermons and crusades and evangelism strategy. In whatever town our crusade or appearance was in, I checked out the courses, plotted the days we would play each, and determined the course records. I looked forward to the next day's round while sitting on the platform waiting to preach.

God's letting me do this because I never got to do it before, I kept telling myself. Something that was bruised inside me needed to be healed. When I drove by a golf course, as much lust and passion to do something as could rise up in a man rose up in me. No cocaine addict was ever more addicted to coke than I was to having fun. I was a fun junkie. I needed it, wanted it, lived for it. My work, my ministry, I am so ashamed to say, was secondary to my full-time job: competing in sports.

When I hit bad shots, I was intolerable. I threw clubs. I smashed more than one driver and not a few putters against trees. Once I was playing with Dave Reagan, a Christian who was on the Professional Golfers' Association tour, and I was down by a stroke or two. I laid a ball up on the green, close to the cup, which would mean an easy putt for a birdie, while his approach shot landed on the edge of the green. As soon as he tried his putt, I could sink mine and edge closer to his score. But he was witnessing to the greenskeeper in the sandtrap.

"C'mon, man!" I nudged. "Let's go! Let's go!"

With horror, I have to admit that when I went to bug him again and realized that he and the man were praying together, I was irritated because the delay was going to get me off pace, take me out of my rhythm, and make me miss the putt for standing around. The man who once promised Jesus that he would always come back and worship Him, the young hotshot evangelist who had supposedly dedicated his life to the winning of souls, was more interested in his golf game than a man's eternal destiny. It's terrible to be that way, but I was hooked.

The man got saved in the sandtrap, but no thanks to me. Even then I knew I was in trouble.

Over the next few years, Betty and I were told that we couldn't have any more children, so in 1969 we adopted James Randall Robison when he was four days old. We called him Randy. Three years later, Betty proved the doctors wrong and gave us our third child, Robin Rochelle Robison. So we had

Rhonda, Randy, and Robin, and Rhonda Renee would eventually grow up and marry Terry Redmon, so she's keeping all those *R*'s rolling.

With our beautiful children, Betty and I should have been deliriously happy in the service of the Lord. But I was the same way at home as I was on the golf course or the tennis court. I could be compassionate and loving, and I could be quick with an apology, but I had a temper and I was in command, in charge, running the show. I loved my kids and my wife, but I could be unkind and harsh to the point that I was capable of psychologically bruising my family—and sometimes I did. No one doubted my salvation or my basic commitment to ministry, but I was no model husband or father. Everyone knew something was wrong, myself included, but none of us could put a finger on it.

The beginning of a turning point came when Peter Lord, the pastor of a large Baptist church, spoke at one of my Bible conferences. Clearly, he was a man of God, a man of the Word. He had a fresh message, and as I sat on the front row listening to him, I knew he was real. He seemed to be free, something I wanted desperately to be. He was honest. He was a devoted pastor, yet he said he had failed with one son, who was a drug addict. His wife had had a nervous breakdown. Another child didn't want to believe in God.

Peter Lord said he had told God, "If this is all there is to it, I quit." He was so honest and real and transparent, I knew I was hearing someone who was speaking the truth. He talked about how God had made us to be like Jesus. He said he had realized that he was not like Jesus. "Are you like Jesus tonight?" he asked the audience. "Anyone?" The question hung in the air. I thought I could ignore it because this was my conference and he was not talking to me. I was on the front row. Surely he was only addressing the audience.

Then he turned his attention toward me. His eyes stopped on me. "Are you like Jesus?" I couldn't respond. I couldn't nod, couldn't shake my head, couldn't do anything. This was too close to home. Was I like Jesus? How long had it been since I could say I was anywhere near to being like Jesus?

Peter was still staring at me. "Are you like Jesus?" The audience chuckled. He had put the host on the spot. I smiled thinly and shook my head from side to side. It was the correct response, humbly admitting that no, not even I was like Jesus. "Perhaps," he continued, "I should ask your wife or your kids if you're like Jesus."

And I thought, *Why ask them?* I could think of so many ways that I wasn't like Jesus. So many inconsistencies, so much self-seeking. I wondered, *What if he asked Rhonda?* She would have to say, "Sir, sometimes my daddy's not at all like Jesus."

Peter Lord and I had breakfast the next morning, and he admitted that one of his problems had been lust. But he said, "God freed me. I didn't think anybody could be free of it. It was ruining my life. But I'm free."

I want to tell you, that got my attention. I got to thinking, *Oh, boy, I'd like to think that'd be possible. To be free, truly free.* Peter was the first person to talk to me about demonic powers, bondage, and deliverance. It scared me, and I'm sure it scared the enemy. Satan didn't want me exposed to it because he knew he had a hook in me, whether I knew it or not. He had a stronghold and was able to control me. He didn't want me free.

Peter ministered to me. He still does, and I just love him. He's honest and open and real. He hears God and tells you what God is saying to him, and he can show it to you in the Word. His abilities are very special. I believe he is anointed to minister to the anointed. He was the first to help me realize not only that something was seriously wrong, but also that something could be done about it.

108

I didn't change, but I started talking about it. I took to saying, to anyone who would listen, "I'm not like Jesus, but I'm going to be. I'm going to get right." If I said that once, I said it dozens of times a week. Finally, one day, after I had repeated that several times, T. D. Hall caught me up short. We were driving away from a meeting, and he had heard enough.

"I keep hearing you say that you're not like Jesus but that you're going to be," he said. "I think you're a hypocrite. I'm tired of hearing you say you're *going* to be. *When* are you going to be? I don't believe you anymore."

Boy, that shook me up. I said silently, "Lord, something's got to change in my life." Religion rather than Christianity was the thing that I detested, yet its trappings had me in its grip. I was going through the motions. I didn't know what had happened to my relationship with Christ, but I knew it was in bad shape. I could remember when I was a teenager and had been consumed with a love for Jesus. Now I was just religious. I was a big-time preacher who loved God, down deep, but this love had faded— it wasn't fresh and personal and vibrant and real.

The same week that T. D. challenged me either to become like Jesus or to quit talking about it, I had an experience with God that almost turned me around for good. We were leaving a pastors' conference in Greenville, South Carolina, when a shy, timid, pale pastor approached me. His polyester pants were shiny, his socks showing thin, his shoes badly worn. "Reverend Robison?"

I paused. "Yes, sir," I responded, condescending to treat him as an equal.

He smiled. "Preacher, I just want you to know that I watch you on television ever' chance I get, and I see you as a prophet. I just wanted to tell you that I love you and I pray for you."

"Well, thank you, Brother. I appreciate that. And you're pastoring where?"

"Oh, just up the road here, sir. We have a little flock of about thirty. We all watch you, and we admire your preaching."

"Thank you very much."

I turned, slid into the passenger side of the front seat, and as Dave Meckley, my sound engineer, pulled away, the Lord spoke to me. "James, did you look at that preacher? Did you see him?"

"Yes, Lord."

"Did you see his shirt?"

"Yes."

"It was cheap, wasn't it?"

"Yeah."

"You've got a nice shirt, don't you?"

"Yes, Lord."

"Did you see his slacks?"

"Yeah."

"They were wrinkled, weren't they?"

"Very wrinkled."

"Yours are pressed, aren't they?"

"Yeah."

"Did you see his shoes?"

"Yes, Lord."

"They had a hole in them, didn't they?"

"Yes."

"You've got nice shoes, don't you?"

"Yeah, I do."

"Did you hear how many people he preaches to on Sunday?"

"He said thirty."

"How many do you preach to, James?"

"I don't know. Perhaps millions."

"You know what, James?"

"What, Lord?"

"*He loves Me,* and *you don't.* And you make Me sick."

With that I laid my head on the dashboard and wept all the

way to the hotel. That little ol' country preacher loved Jesus with all his heart, and I didn't. It just tore me up. I wanted to come back to God. I knew I needed a time of brokenness, and God really did break me. I confessed to the Lord that I didn't love Him like I should. I cried and cried, and then I called Betty. "Honey," I said, "I just got right with God."

She began to weep. "That's great, James."

Rhonda asked Betty what was the matter. "Daddy's just got right with God," Betty said.

"I thought Daddy was always right with God."

"Well, he'll have to explain it to you."

When I got home, I did just that. I told her, "I just hadn't loved Jesus with all my heart. And I want to."

I wanted that experience to make a difference. I really did. I tried to reform. I made progress, but it didn't last.

Prisoner in the Promised Land

In a matter of months, I was back at the same level of despair. I felt trapped. I seemed to have no hope. I had no fresh relationship with God through Christ. I had to fake my vitality, my zeal.

My citywide crusades, meanwhile, were booming. Five, six, ten thousand people a night. I remembered the days when I used to kneel with the local committee and my staff for a half-hour before a meeting, beseeching God to anoint me with His Holy Spirit, to prepare hearts and minds for the message, to give me the words to say, to convict me of sin, to take away my pride, to make me a pure vessel, to keep me from getting in the way. Only when I felt I had had a good time before the Father did I feel confident to be His messenger.

Then I took to kneeling briefly, usually alone, and saying, "God, anoint me and use me. Lord, I love You." Then it got to the point that I just pleaded with the Lord to use me in spite of myself. Before I knew it, I was pausing only briefly at the door to the platform or hesitating an instant behind the curtain to breathe a prayer. Finally, I had come full circle. I was honest. "Lord," I would pray as I strode toward the platform, "I don't even want to go out there. I don't even want to preach. Please let somebody else do it." I went days and days without even reading my Bible. I used the same sermons again and again. I was miserable.

My relationship with Betty was strained. Many times, she wept and said, "James, I want things to be right." But she had heard me literally pray that I would die.

"Betty, I don't care if I never preach again. It's like something's got hold of my brain. Like a claw has my mind in its clutches. I'm living in such defeat I can't stand it. It's like my mind's on fire. I can't control my thoughts. I can't control my appetite." I was gaining weight at an alarming rate, though most couldn't tell because of my height. "Betty, I wish you'd pray that I would die in my sleep."

Of course, that was the last thing in the world she wanted to do. If anything, *she* wanted to die. She felt responsible. She felt she wasn't the right kind of wife for an evangelist; somehow, she felt, she was one of the causes of my misery.

In the midst of my big ministry and my personal, spiritual drought, God revealed to me that *most* preachers experience similar problems. Talk about burnout, despair, and depression! I didn't want to go on anymore. Though we had recently moved into a nice new home and my wife and children were precious and beautiful, everything in my life seemed dull and dead. I pleaded with God, "What's going on?"

I knew I had everything to be happy about. A successful ministry. Big crowds. A large growing multimillion dollar budget. Great results. And yet I did not want to live. I didn't believe it was possible for a Christian to really live in victory. During the next few months, the devil came against me as an angel of light. He made me every kind of promise. He told me what he was going to do for me, and he sounded like God. But he was denying Scripture. He was offering things—fame, glory, prestige, money—I had no business desiring. He was contradicting the Word of God. I could hear the devil communicating directly with me. I sensed his power over me.

Suddenly he tried to beguile me with temptation such as I never before experienced. I began to have lust that was beyond anything I had ever known. I knew it was dangerous, but I felt almost helpless to fight it. Praise God, I did fight it and never succumbed to my thoughts because I knew it would destroy me and my ministry, but what a battle!

In talking with my contemporaries and associates, I found out that it was the same way with them. How discouraging! It seemed there was no solution, no chance of really living free. "Oh God," I prayed, "it didn't used to be this way. Does this have to be the norm? What's going on?"

I took some refuge in being honest with Dudley Hall. I would call him and ask him, in different ways, "Dudley, can you be free? Can a person really be free? Can you? Can I? What has to happen to free us from this kind of stuff in our minds?"

Dudley tried to give me comfort, yet he couldn't come right out and say, "Yes, I know you can be free." The problem was that this was new to me. I was encountering direct spiritual attack from a realm I had been taught to ignore. There was sin, sure. There was a devil, yes. But those were concepts, the opposites of God, something to be shunned, prayed about, dealt with, and forgotten. I could hardly bring myself to think that Satan's power in the realm of darkness and deception and destruction was so keen that the activity was literal and powerfully real to me every day.

I had preached many times that we wrestle not, as the apostle Paul says, with flesh and blood, but with powers and principalities, yet it hadn't even soaked into my own head. The devil has taught us to ignore him. I ignored him and found my life filled with the fiery darts of the wicked one. I was being ground under his heel.

While sitting on the platform at my meetings or even while preaching, I might become aware of a woman watching me. If I returned her gaze, a powerful force field between us seemed to draw her to me and me to her. I was filled with lustful thoughts and desires even while sitting on the platform at a crusade or at church.

And it wasn't as if this was all in my imagination. It was real. After the meeting, the women often sought me out, on the platform, in the parking lot, or even sometimes at my hotel. They might have appeared to be high-class, attractive women, even wives of spiritual men, but they had felt what I had felt. Usually I ran the other way and wouldn't even talk with them, but when—on occasion—I was forced to make conversation, they often let me know of their availability to me. That had never happened to me before, but it started happening regularly—a different one in each city or even one at each meeting. I was terrified of the possibilities and of the direct attack on me.

Betty was overwhelmed by fear. The devil pointed out to her all the women who would be better for me than she was. They might be sophisticated or confident or articulate, and Satan would say, "See? She's the kind of wife James needs." Betty prepared herself to die because she was convinced that God would take her so I could have a more outgoing woman for a wife. She was quiet and shy and felt she had no talent. That precious little girl who is so sweet and has always been the only love of my life was convinced by the devil that she was going to die in her early thirties. He was working on my family, trying to destroy me and everything around me. That's how he operates.

I tried to pray. I tried to repent. But it seemed as if I had gone past the point of no return. I went through very temporary times of release. I would feel as if my repentance had been real, and I'd think I was getting better. But something was pulling the strings, dragging me down. I was bound.

I didn't realize at the time that my experience paralleled the power of the enemy as illustrated in the Old Testament when the Israelites built strongholds in Israel. In Habakkuk 1 you can read where people were dragged into bondage, though they were in the Promised Land. They found themselves prisoners at the hand of the enemy *while they were in the Promised Land*. (See Nehemiah 9 and Psalm 78.)

Every one of them was involved in religious ceremonies. Each was making a sacrifice, going to the temple, burning incense, praying, giving, tithing. Yet they lived in absolute defeat. Many, of course, were rebelling in disobedience, but many—like me— were going through the motions of their religious beliefs. A person doesn't have to be living in open rebellion to be in bondage.

I was doing everything right, but my heart was away from God. My heart was divided. I had to do what was expected of me. I was a prisoner of religious spirits and many others. I couldn't move. I couldn't hear God. I had to be sure to do what my peers expected me to do. I said I was doing what God wanted me to do, but in fact, I was succumbing to the pressures of men and allowing myself to seek their approval. I didn't realize what was happening, though.

I wasn't forgiving people I was unhappy with. I wouldn't get right with them. Jesus says you'll be turned over to the tormentors if you don't forgive. I was not forgiving. I had let resentment build in my life, and I was being destroyed. My physical body was in such torment that doctors couldn't give me enough medicine to mask the pain. I constantly went to them for relief, but I couldn't seem to get better.

My problem was deeper than they, or even I, knew. I was drained of energy, sapped of strength. I was in pitiful condition, and I didn't want to go on. Coming home from a crusade one night with just an associate in the plane with me, I pointed the twin-engine plane toward the ground and let it fall. He was not a pilot, so he didn't know what to do except to plead with me and pull back on the controls. If it hadn't been for some shred of decency that told me it would be unfair to make him and his family suffer because of my despair, I wouldn't have brought that plane back under control. If I had been alone, I would likely have become an airplane crash victim, dying in east Texas, not far from where Ricky Nelson died a few years later.

I had come to the end of myself physically, emotionally, mentally, and spiritually. I was a living dead man.

The seeds of defeat and destruction had grown into ugly, briarlike fruit in my life. I became so much like a thorn hedge, as the Old Testament says, that you couldn't stand to get close to me. I'd cut you. I'd pierce your heart.

Praise God, He loves us even when we're defeated. Some folks don't believe that, and it'll rattle some preachers' theology, too, but God loves us even when we're in rebellion. Oh, make no mistake, our rebellion will cost us. It nearly cost me everything. My lack of interest in Him and my lack of love and intensity for His will cost me and hurt me. But He loved me still.

Nothing could separate me from His love.

117

CHAPTER 16

Rally for Freedom

Ironically, while I was in the depths of despair in my spiritual life and walk with the Lord, and while my wife was terrified about what lay ahead for her, her husband, and her family, I was involved in the first of two dynamic, victorious episodes in my ministry.

Early in 1979, when I was a dark-visaged, angry preacher who felt as if he was living a lie, I taped one of my television shows, and it was released as usual to stations all over the country. It had the standard mix of music, a personal challenge from me directly to the viewer, an enthusiastic sermon, and an offer to our friends in exchange for their love gifts. It was the general program we had found successful, not apologizing for the money appeal because we were not interrupting with commercials every few minutes.

If someone had said, "James, you're gonna get in trouble for that program," and made me guess why and from which station the heat would come, I would have been at a loss. In retrospect, it's easy to see, but back then I never questioned my right as an American to the freedom of speech. I believed then, and I believe now, that anyone in this country is free to state any opinion he wants about anything or anybody, as long as he doesn't slander or defame an individual.

In that program I spoke briefly and pointedly about the sin of homosexuality. I said that the Bible is clear that the practicing homosexual will not enter the kingdom of God. Then I quoted a Los Angeles police chief who had said that some homosexuals were dangerous because they preyed on one another. I wasn't excited at the time. I wasn't shouting. It was a casual program, but I was definite. I called homosexuality what the Bible calls it: a sin, a perversion, a wrong.

Now, of course, it's easy to see why some militant gay group might be offended by that, but you probably wouldn't guess that the opposition came from a local station in Dallas, WFAA–Channel 8, one of my strongest outlets. Not only did they kick me off the air, but they also gave the homosexuals equal time. At least they called it equal time. They narrowed my offensive statements to the portion in which I related the comments of the police chief, about twenty seconds. In exchange for that, the gays got a half-hour to refute me.

After much prayer, I began my fight to get back on the air by playing the underdog. I developed a bumper sticker that showed an American flag and a TV in one corner with the message: FREEDOM OF SPEECH, THE RIGHT TO PREACH. That bumper sticker seemed to show up on every car in the Dallas Metroplex!

I made it clear that I had been whipped. I had been forced off the air. The big TV stations, the communications moguls owned the little preacher. The Dallas Christian community was up in arms. The manager of the TV station came out of a restaurant one day to find our bumper stickers on his car.

119

When the issue first came up I went to Dave Lane, a WFAA executive. "You've made a mistake," I told him. "If you're going to get on me, don't do it over this issue, because it's going to cost you. The people of Dallas will not put up with this, and I won't take it sitting down either. This is the number one station in my home area, and I just can't let it go without a fight."

When it became clear that the station was not going to put our program back on the air, we hired the great criminal lawyer, Richard "Racehorse" Haynes. He had never lost a case. Having a lawyer who became famous in big murder cases made headlines everywhere. Why was he interested? "Because," he said, "this is a constitutional issue."

The crisis polarized the Christian community all over the country. I got a letter from Pat Robertson, telling me, "You're the man to fight this fight. It's about time somebody did." Many well-known and not-so-well-known preachers wrote to tell me they thought I was the ambassador to give preaching its due as a constitutional right. The problem became a springboard for Christians who realized that if they didn't do something, they could eventually lose their freedom to worship.

Our opposition to Channel 8's decision rallied Christians from all denominations and culminated in a Freedom Rally in Dallas on June 5, 1979, organized by Freddie Gage. Twelve thousand people jammed a local auditorium! Channel 8 sent a cameraman who fed a live picture back to the owners and staff and sponsors at the studios, and we knew they had to fear that we would storm their place. Of course, no one intended anything of the kind. What a glorious night it was!

The enthusiasm ran high, and people had a righteous cause in their hearts. All evening the speakers were interrupted with thunderous ovations and cheers and amens. Pastors and leaders representing the independent Baptist churches, the Southern Baptists, the Church of the Nazarene, the Assemblies of God,

Methodists, Church of God, Pentecostal, several black denominations, Lutherans, Catholics, Episcopalians, Church of Christ, Jews, and many others stood with us in the fight for freedom.

Howard Phillips, national director of the Conservative Caucus in Washington, D. C., was the first to speak. He reminded the noisy crowd that "the founders of our great country [knew] that our rights did not come from government, they came from God. The authors of the Declaration of Independence said that we were endowed by our *Creator* with certain unalienable rights. . . ."

He made the point that homosexuality was not only a crime against society, but also a crime against God. "These are *not* victimless crimes. . . . Homosexuality is wrong; it is something to be stamped out rather than something to be celebrated. . . . Shall a preacher have the right to preach what he believes? Shall a preacher have the right to preach what the Bible teaches, or shall government intervene and deny that preacher's right?

"Americans have learned to love and respect the work of Reverend James Robison. We don't want his message to be diluted. We don't want the government or the television stations or the commercial sponsors to be able to say, 'This is what you can preach,' or 'This is what you can't preach.'"

Southern Baptist evangelist J. Harold Smith said, "Brother James, I'm delighted that you got cut off that station. Had it not been for that event, we would not have had this great meeting here tonight. I'm glad that the devil can see in Dallas and this surrounding area that God is still on the throne. I'd like to remind the devil and his crowd that before there was ever a government or a Parliament or a Congress or a Supreme Court of the United States, or a judge or a jury or an attorney, God was.

"So I'm here, first of all, because I love the Lord. Second, because I love this man of God, and I believe what he preaches.

121

You can rest assured that I would not have come here if he was one of those tweedledee, tweedledum, pussyfootin', compromisin', back-scratchin', ear-ticklin' soft-soapers."

Well, that line brought the house down. The place was electric with emotion, with support, with godly indignation. Brother Smith finished by saying that he would rather be "run over by a bulldozer, I'd rather be a dead dog in the street than be one of these preachers that doesn't believe that this Book is the inspired, infallible Word of God. Long after all the enemies of this Book have become buzzard meat, this Bible will still be, and the Word of God shall prevail."

Our lawyer, Mr. Haynes, asked the crowd, "Do you think it's fair that our children be daily exposed to salacious sexuality and matter-of-fact violence on TV? Do you think it's fair that TV speaks *of* evil and *about* evil but will not let James speak out *against* evil? How can that be fair? It can't be!"

Jerry Falwell, pastor of the Thomas Road Baptist Church, Lynchburg, Virginia, and chancellor of Liberty University, said, "This is not a matter of homosexuality. Nothing so trivial as that. In very simple terms, homosexuality is perversion. It always has been. It ever shall be. And there is no point in addressing the matter.

"Freedom of speech and freedom of religion and the freedom to voice our moral convictions—that is a conviction with us and we will not back up. We will not give ground."

Pastor of the First Baptist Church of Dallas, Rev. W. A. Criswell, said: "Who owns the airwaves? God made them, and He made them for all the people." He challenged the two innocent local TV stations to "champion the people, to be a friend of the churches of the living Lord, to refuse to be intimidated by a minuscule, insignificant, inconsequential bunch of sexual perverts, and invite Robison onto the airwaves!" The people leaped to their feet.

Criswell continued, "And while you're standing, let me say a word to Channel 8! If you are proud of the decision that you have made, I challenge you and dare you to call a national convention of the perverts that you champion and see if you like the friends you've made and the company you keep!

"In the heart of the Apocalypse, the sainted apostle John sees an angel flying through the midst of the heavens, having the everlasting gospel to preach. If the wings of that angel are clipped and he can no longer fly, then, Lord God, give the message to James Robison, and he will proclaim it to the ends of the earth! This is James Robison!"

Finally, after two hours of music, messages, an offering, and testimonies, it was my turn. My throat was sore, my voice sounded terrible. "Words are inadequate to express enough gratitude to all of you and to all of these men who have preceded me tonight. This is not an assembly in my honor. We're not here to pay tribute to James Robison. We are here in honor of almighty God, His Word, and our Constitution. I am not flattered, but yes, I am deeply grateful to God for the manifestation of such support. My dear friends, the Spirit that prevails in this assembly is the only hope this nation and the world has for survival.

"It is an answer to my prayer to see different denominations here—those who believe the Bible. And if you do not believe the Bible, we have no basis for fellowship. And by believing the Bible, I mean believing that it is the inerrant, infallible, inspired Word of the living, eternal God, that it's God-breathed, and that it must be proclaimed without apology in the power of the Holy Spirit. To see you come together and to love the Lord and His Word and to love one another is a deep inspiration to me, and I want to thank God and thank you for the privilege of such a sight.

"It is my prayer that WFAA will rescind its horrendous, tragic decision and put us back on the air. I ask you to pray that we might have in this community someone humble enough, honest enough to admit, 'We made a mistake, and we want to correct it in the name of freedom, liberty, and justice. We don't care who doesn't like it; we believe it's right, and we want to do it. We'll put him back on the air.' That's my prayer.

"Someone has asked me if, on this occasion, I still believe that homosexuality is a sin. My dear friends, homosexuality was a sin when God almighty rained fire on Sodom and Gomorrah. It was a sin when Paul penned the letter to the Romans and to the Corinthians. It was a sin on February 25, 1979, when I preached that it was sin on WFAA–Channel 8 in Dallas. It is a sin on June 5, 1979, in Dallas, and it will be a sin until Jesus comes again.

"It is perversion of the highest order. It is against God, against God's Word, against society, and against nature. It is almost too repulsive to imagine and describe. It is filth. God have mercy upon homosexuals. The Bible is not against homosexuals, but it speaks specifically against the sin of homosexuality. It also speaks against the sin of complacency. God deliver us as Christians from apathy, indifference, and complacency, or we're all dead.

"I was preaching from Romans, chapter 1, when I lost access to the airwaves. I wonder who under heaven or who out of hell may now come and try to stop an assembly such as this as I again shall speak from Romans, chapter 1. There is only one way they can silence these lips, and that's to bury me six feet beneath the earth. Bless God, at the Rapture I'll come out of the grave preaching Romans, chapter 1—homosexuality is still a sin.

"How on earth can some denominations be so foolhardy as to convene and vote on whether or not homosexuality is a sin when God settled it long ago? I declare to you, I do not care if they drag all Ten Commandments of the almighty God into the political arena. I will still preach 'Thus sayeth the Lord God . . .' and if the Supreme Court decides that hell is cruel and unusual punishment, I will still stand up and preach what the Bible says about hell! There is a hell!

"You may say, 'James Robison, you're a troublemaker.' Well, you're right. I'm worse than a troublemaker; I'm a reactionary. I react. I react to the burning of the American flag. I react to the assassination attempts on the Constitution of the United States. I react to the bureaucratic overregulations in this country, to the violations of the rights of the American people, to the tax-paid private lobbyists, to the invasion of my privacy and of the privacy of any other American.

"I react to war supported for financial gain, to irresponsible voting in Congress, to the blatant compromise with communism, to prayer removed from our schools. I react to murder in the name of abortion, to abortion in the name of women's rights. I react! I react when homosexuality is labeled a normal lifestyle. I react to sex out of wedlock. I react to the abuses of little children, to crime and violence on television, to the new morality—which is immorality. I react to welfare over work, to preachers who won't preach, to churches who have no mission, to pornography in the name of art, to the excessive and unnecessary taxation of the American people. I react to pot parties over birthday parties. I react to worthless politicians over statesmanship. I react to the loss of the freedoms granted us by the Constitution, and brother, I'm ready to do something about it.

"The blackest day in human history may soon dawn in Dallas. A president died here without our consent. But freedom of religion and freedom of speech will only die here with the silent consent of indifferent Christians and Americans. If we lose here, we lose all over America. We cannot let it happen. It must not happen.

"The person who registered the complaint against me didn't

125

even see the program. *One* person complained. One person, and a million people can't hear the Bible preached as it is to men as they are. God help us. The station manager who put me off the air hadn't even seen the program. He watched it with me the day after he kicked me off the air. The first thing he said to me was that I couldn't say homosexuality is a sin because it's not against the law.

"He's since found out that it is against the law, but I don't care whether it's against man's law or not; it's against God's law, and I'm obliged to preach God's law. They told me I couldn't preach against abortion. I couldn't preach on a woman's place in the home. But I have to preach what the Bible says. Friends, we've got to stand up and say, 'This is right,' and if it costs me my life, I'm gonna stand for what's right. And that goes for television stations. Stand up for what's right.

"We've got to take a stand, and I plead with you to join us. If I lose this case, brother, if they can put me off the air because I represent one side of the issue, then I'll never have to pay for any more television time in my life because I'm gonna bring suits against every program that goes against what I believe as a Christian, and I want equal time! Give it to me, in the name of the Lord!

"Someone says, 'Well, preachers ought not mess with politics,' but brother, when a preacher does his business, he messes with everything. I want to say something to you mealy-mouthed preachers that are in the crowd tonight. There's a few of you who slipped in to see what was being said, and you're getting an earful. You listen to me. If your preaching doesn't affect the thinking, the living, the talking, the acting, the lifestyle, and the voting of the people sitting in your church, you'd better vacate the pulpit because it's full of sounding brass and tinkling cymbals. Get out of it!

"Nothing greater ever happens in a city than when God's man

gets up and preaches God's Word. If you believe anything's more important than that, go do it. There's nothing more noble than preaching. Preach it, preach God's Word, not your own opinion.

"Why am I here?

"To *Announce* my intentions to maintain our freedom.

"To *Blast* the avowed enemies of freedom.

"To *Challenge* the assassins of freedom.

"To *Demand* the rights of our freedom. To *Dedicate* ourselves to the noble cause of freedom.

"To *Enlist* an army of defenders of freedom. To *Enlighten* minds concerning the tragic loss of freedom. . . .

"*Protect* our freedom. *Proclaim* our freedom. *Plead* the case of freedom. *Plow up* the plotters against freedom.

"*Question* the decisions hindering freedom.

"*Restate* the story of freedom. *Report* the injustices against freedom. *Resist* the theft of our freedom. . . .

"*Yell* for the cause of freedom.

"And *Zero* in on the destroyers of freedom. That's why I'm here tonight.

"When America gets too intelligent for God, she's become unintelligent. When she gets too big for God, she's too big. And when she divorces herself from God, she will crumble in the dust. When America forsakes the guidance of God, she's dead.

"The greatest problem in our country is that it is no longer under God. It's our responsibility to call our people back to God. We must not lose freedom. America will be the land of the free only as long as it's the home of the brave.

"No man on this earth can put a noose around God's preachers. If we allow a decision to stand, such as the one WFAA made, then I believe that everyone in Dallas has sanctioned their decision. How can you put a preacher off the air for preaching the truth, for preaching the Bible? I'm sick of being quiet! I'm sick of being silent! I'm sick of the godless, unholy

127

actions some people take. It's time to reverse some decisions. They can parade their naked women and burlesque queens, but we can't preach the sweet message of Jesus? God knows somebody has got to present the other side of the picture. Will you join your hearts, your hands, your lives, and will you march to change America for the glory of God?"

Later, with the help of Mary Crowley and the women of First Baptist Church in Dallas, the matter was settled out of court. I was soon back on the air.

When Mother decided it would be better for someone else to raise me, she placed this ad in the Houston newspaper.

Because we moved five or six times a year when I first went to live with Mother, wherever we lived did not seem like home.

*I was eight years old
at Wooldridge
Elementary.*

*Long-time friend, Billy Foote, and I, spring 1962. Billy gave me my first
public opportunity to share the love of Christ.*

One of many informal youth meetings held in the 1960s and 1970s.

Area crusade, Oklahoma City, 1967.

James with Dale Evans.

James Robison, W. A. Criswell, Jerry Falwell (l. to r.). Dr. Criswell and Reverend Falwell were key speakers at the Freedom Rally, June 5, 1979.

James with Johnny and June Carter Cash.

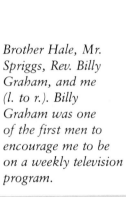

Brother Hale, Mr. Spriggs, Rev. Billy Graham, and me (l. to r.). Billy Graham was one of the first men to encourage me to be on a weekly television program.

Twenty-five thousand attended the 1975 crusade in Mobile, Alabama.

President-elect Ronald Reagan, 1979. I spent a lot of time in Washington in 1980, trying to get to know and influence the presidential candidates.

Although I supported Reagan for the Republican presidential nominee, I felt confident George Bush would become his running mate. Here we are at the White House in 1981.

Here I am with my wife, Betty, Mrs. Reagan, and President Reagan, 1982.

Mom and Dad Hale gave me a home and led me to Christ. I knew they loved me.

Yet Another Triumph

That same year, 1979, despite the bankruptcy of my personal spiritual life, I enjoyed a privilege few men on the face of the earth will ever enjoy. I was invited to join several Christian leaders for two days of private prayer in a hotel at the Dallas/Fort Worth Airport.

What a group of godly men! My pastor, Jimmy Draper, went with me, and we talked and prayed with Charles Stanley, Adrian Rogers, Billy Graham, Bill Bright, Pat Robertson, Rex Humbard, James Kennedy, and Clayton Bell. It was one of the most special times of my life.

Out of those discussions grew great support for the massive Washington for Jesus Rally and its evolving from being an exclusively charismatic function to a broad-based evangelical meeting. I felt honored that I had the chance to encourage that support, along with encouraging my friends, Adrian Rogers and Charles Stanley to speak. Then Bill Bright and I joined the executive steering committee.

It was an incredible two-day experience, being on the inside, listening to those great men of God share their hearts, their concerns, their fears, their hopes. They debated; they argued; they prayed together. At one point, Charles Stanley said, "I'll die to preach the truth about the Christian's political responsibility. I will not back down."

Billy Graham countered, "I won't again become involved with politics. I've been burned so badly with my relationship with leaders that I'm going to just preach the gospel."

"I'll die for it, Billy," Dr. Stanley repeated.

As much as I love and respect and admire Billy Graham, I had to take Charles's side in that discussion. "We have to get the Christian involved, or we won't have a future."

"Oh, I agree with that," Billy said. "God has shown me that we have less than a thousand days left as a free nation if we do not see some sort of an awakening."

Bill Bright was alarmed. "That is the precise message God has given me, too," he said. "Three years if something doesn't happen."

Adrian Rogers agreed. "If we don't see a turn, we won't have anywhere to preach the gospel."

We went from that place with a message to the nation, to Christians. We were saying that it was time to get involved, to march on Washington, to back up the march with prayer, to turn the nation back to God. The Washington for Jesus Rally was a huge success, and by the time it was over, the Christian community in this country was eager to get on to the next presidential election. In 1980, the front runners would be the incumbent Democrat Jimmy Carter and Republican Ronald Reagan.

I spent a lot of time in Washington getting to know the leaders and trying to influence them. When I wasn't there, I was preaching all over the country. Annually, I spoke at Jerry Falwell's church and school, as well as encouraging Moral Majority meetings. Meanwhile, my Texas-based Bible conference ministry had proved to be the most visible pulpit for the many leaders of the Southern Baptist Convention. It was a way for them to reach the people outside their own churches on a wide scale. Adrian Rogers, Bailey Smith, James Draper, Charles Stanley—all of them became much more widely known through our Bible conferences as we televised them.

I saw people saved and join churches all over the nation. The Southern Baptists and many other groups saw me as influential in their churches and denominations. Not only was I adding to their rolls, I was also visible, a mover and shaker in the political arena. I was serious about getting Christians more involved in national politics, and I dreamed of getting the major candidates to address what I would call a National Affairs Briefing of several thousand patriotic evangelicals in Dallas early in the election year.

I was convinced that Ronald Reagan would become the next president of the United States. I was absolutely certain of it. I tried to meet with John B. Anderson and Jimmy Carter and did meet with George Bush, John Conolly, and a few others, but after I met with Reagan, there was no changing my mind.

Early in 1980 I met with Reagan in Atlanta along with Adrian Rogers, and a few others. Later I told Reagan of my dream to give the Christian community a chance to hear all the candidates, and I figured that the only way to get all of them to come would be to ensure that the leading candidate would be there. "That will be you, of course," I said.

He smiled. "I certainly hope so, Reverend Robison." He explained that he was well aware of the interest of the Christian public in politics, as evidenced by Jimmy Carter's victory over Gerald Ford, who had edged Reagan for the Republican nomination in 1976.

I asked him, "Mr. Reagan, is the Lord real to you?"

131

"Well, my mother introduced me to the Lord. As a child, I became a Christian."

I pressed. "But is He real to you? Is Jesus really real to you?"

"As real as my mother."

"You mean your relationship with Jesus is as real to you as your relationship with your mother?"

"Yes. Just like with my mother. He's that real."

A few months later I communicated with Governor Reagan. He assured me that if I would set it up, get it rolling, and produce a crowd in Dallas that would hear him and any other candidate who wished to come, he would be there. We scheduled our briefing for the Reunion Arena, which held seventeen thousand, for August, after the Republican National Convention. Our hope was that Anderson and Carter would appear, too.

During the preparations for the big meeting, my views became known. I was labeled a conservative Christian, backing Ronald Reagan. That didn't sit well with fellow Texan and presidential hopeful George Bush. He used a mild profane expression in the press about not caring who the ultraconservatives backed, and it was a mistake—one of several in his short-lived campaign.

I wrote him and chided him about his profanity and about not caring what conservatives thought. He immediately sent back a handwritten note acknowledging that I was right and that he stood corrected. When he eventually dropped out of the race, however, he still took shots at me and those like me.

Late in the spring, I had already gotten Reagan's commitment to join us after the convention, so I was in frequent contact with him. But I still felt it was necessary to set things straight with George Bush. The day after he dropped out of the race, I flew to Houston and called him, asking if he'd see me.

He seemed surprised and a little flustered, but he agreed. When I walked into his office, I found him looking tired, worn out from a grueling campaign. He reminded me a little of me. His sleeves were rolled up, he was casual, and he was laid back, enjoying the break. "I can't believe you came all the way down here," Mr. Bush said. "What are you doing here?"

I got right to the point as I sat down. "Obviously, you and I are poles apart as far as you're concerned, but let me tell you what I believe and let's see if you don't think we are closer than you might have thought. I care about my country. I believe you care about your country. Since we both want what's best for America, it seems to me it would be good if we could communicate so we might understand each other. Maybe I see things that would help you, and maybe you see things that would help me.

"I don't see how two men can do their country much good if they won't even communicate. So, what I'm here to tell you is that I care about you. Although I didn't believe you were the right man for the presidency, I do believe you're going to be vice president."

"Well, James," he said, "I'm not going to accept any call to the vice presidency, should one come, and I doubt it will."

"That's today," I said with a smile. "At the convention, you'll take it."

"No, I won't either."

"Yes, you will. I'm convinced you're going to be vice president of the United States, and that means you're going to be one heartbeat from the presidency. So, since I care about my country enough to be involved, I'm here to tell you that I love you, I care about you, and I want to communicate with you. I don't want a barrier to be between us. If you would, I'd like for us to kneel right here and pray together."

He stood. "I can hardly believe this. I want you to know I'm impressed. Yes, sir, I'll pray with you."

We knelt right there in his office, and from that moment to this, I feel we've been good friends.

As I predicted, Reagan won the Republican nomination in a walk, and Bush accepted the running mate position. Following the convention and near to the fall elections, we had our meeting at the Reunion Arena. Only Reagan was there, but we had preachers and well-known evangelical leaders from all over, plus enough lay people to fill the arena. Mr. Reagan knew that we were not a body who planned to make any endorsements; we were just there to listen and to consider the issues. He accepted my suggested opening and began by saying, "You can't endorse me, but I endorse you."

That endeared him to the assembly and he was off and running. Four hundred members of the media, including representatives of all the major networks and newsweeklies, were there. I had designed a pin that simply spelled out *V-O-T-E* with a cross in place of the *T*. That pin made the cover of *Time* and *Newsweek,* and it seemed everyone I knew was wearing one.

If it hadn't been for the problems in my private spiritual life, I would have been on top of the world. I was being lauded as a man who had organized—with the next president of the United States—one of the biggest political meetings in history. I was busy, visible, influential, and politically astute. I could have and should have been in a position to be used of God to do great things, to be victorious, to be an example, to be a great husband and father and Christian and leader and preacher and prophet.

I was sincere and right in my convictions, but in reality, I was personally defeated. I was miserable, more miserable than ever. I was sick, lonely, depressed. I was a prisoner. I often lived for the attention, but then I felt like a hypocrite because I cared too much about myself. My drives, my lusts, my appetite, were out of control. The little good I did, the influence I had, was at times from wrong motives. In my heart I wanted the best for our country, the church and God, but I was still trapped.

Betty was suffering every bit as much as I was. One of the

hardest parts for her was that she could clearly remember how happy and contented we were in the Lord's work during the early days of our marriage. "It was wonderful," she says, "to be in love and to be in a ministry and serving the Lord. But as God blessed, we got busy doing and doing and doing. Soon we found we had less time alone for the Lord and for His Word. I saw the joy leave our home. I saw confusion and misery set in. I saw a husband who would get up into the pulpit and wish he wasn't there. But because God had called him to preach, he felt he had to preach.

"Because I loved him so much, I prayed for him. I interceded for him and asked the Lord to do something in his life to change the way things were. James's and my communication had been wonderful. We loved each other. The Lord had blessed us with three beautiful children. What more could we want? But our hearts weren't in tune with God. I had prayed for three or four years that the Lord would put a special touch upon our home."

I was so consumed with lust by this time that I began to fear for my life and my ministry. I was able to resist, but I feared what might happen if I was approached by a woman when I was alone and weak. Would I, could I, fall? I was scared to death. I didn't know my wife had been praying for me. If I had, I might not have been so surprised when the answer came at long last.

I was so far from an answer in myself that I confided to Dudley Hall and to my wife that I felt as if I was on fire, that my insides were burning. I knew I was in bondage, but I had no idea how to escape. Can a man be truly free? I asked that of Dudley every chance I got. He didn't have a satisfactory answer.

I had given up hope. How could God possibly become as real to me now as he had been when I was a fresh-faced college kid, promising to always love Him and come back to Him and praise Him? I had drifted so far so fast.

I sincerely believed I was out of options.

Free at Last!

It makes me cringe to admit that throughout my preaching ministry, I had made fun of people I felt overemphasized the gifts of the Holy Spirit. It wasn't that I didn't believe the gifts were valid, or even that they weren't manifest today. On the contrary, I was different from most fundamentalists in believing that they *were* for today. In fact, more than once, Jerry Falwell and I had argued that very point.

But from the pulpit, I was basically anticharismatic. I was a Fundamentalist, a Southern Baptist, and I disdained any showy manifestation of the gifts. In one sense, I still disdain that. The gifts are not to be shown off, except to the glory of God. And people are to be wise, not foolish, about them. But the fact remains, I was known as a typical antigifts Fundamentalist preacher, which made my basic Baptist constituencies totally comfortable.

The first hint of a thaw in my attitudes and in my spiritual iciness came on a Saturday morning in Houston in 1980. I was at a large Bible conference on the platform with Bailey Smith, Jerry Falwell, and several other evangelists and leaders. In walked Dudley Hall, my buddy. He was to speak that morning.

Dudley had been at a crusade in Dothan, Alabama, that had broken out into a real revival, several weeks in duration. People were saved, Christians were brought to repentance, and the word was spreading that something special, something real, had happened there. Dudley was a little late getting in, so our meeting had already begun. He tiptoed across the stage and sat next to me, then looked directly into my eyes.

"I'm free."

The words almost didn't reach me, they were so foreign by then. He had heard me ask if a person could be free, really free, for so long that he tried to communicate the new truth in his life in my language. All I could do was look at him and squint.

He repeated his message. "I'm really free, James. I'm really free. Man, I mean, I'm free."

What was playing at the edges of my miserable mind? I sat on that platform trying to look spiritual and pious and even healthy. It took all my strength. And that man had a word of hope I was too far gone to even hear. Hope. He was in the religious world, a colaborer, a cosufferer, a cocaptive, for all I knew. Free.

When it was time for him to preach, I was awe-struck. I saw the evidence! He was anointed. It glowed; it showed; I could see it, hear it, and feel it. The Spirit of God was on the man. He was free indeed! He was different!

Later I asked him what had happened. He gave the credit, after the Lord, to a simple layman who believed the Bible. "The Bible came alive in his life, James. The Word of God tore down the strongholds of the enemy, and he walked in a new freedom and fullness, more than he had ever known before."

"And the same has happened to you?"

"It has."

"I can tell, Dudley. But can it happen to anybody?"

"Anybody, James. It can happen to anybody."

It was too good to be true, but it was hard to argue against physical, human, flesh-and-blood evidence. Still, I argued. I didn't believe it. I fought it. I resisted what had happened in Dudley's life. I criticized the ministry that came from it. Why, because, to me, he was acting like a faith healer!

At first, he was patient. He was kind. He was a good brother, as always. He just quietly told me that I needed to get together with the layman, Milton Green. I decided I would do it, but I wanted to be in charge. It would be on my terms, on my schedule. Sure, I was intrigued. I was interested. But I was also afraid. Was the man going to get too close to the evil world, the supernatural powers? Was I going to be embarrassed, humiliated? Would I be the victim of something I had preached against for years?

I kept calling Dudley, complaining of my bondage, of my misery. Finally, his patience came to an end. "If you don't want to get together with Milton," he told me, "then don't call me anymore with your problems. You're wearing me out and driving me away from the Word with all your talk. Your mouth goes ninety miles an hour and you say nothing, and I can't hear God for listening to you." Dudley hung up on me.

Finally, I called Milt and asked if he would travel with me to a series of meetings in Alabama. He agreed. I didn't ask for an appointment for deliverance. I didn't know what to expect. I just wanted him to go with me without my telling him that I felt I was in trouble, in bondage. On the plane I found myself strangely uncomfortable in his presence. I felt conspicuous, planning my sermons from newspapers and magazines rather than from the Scriptures as I always had in years past.

I assured myself that a big-time evangelist had to know what was going on in the world, but all Milt did—he had a ninth-grade education—was read the Bible and point out Scriptures to me. I'd never seen a Bible like his. Every verse was marked up, and it appeared he had circled every word of every verse. I thought, *This guy's a fanatic; he's really lived with his Bible*. I saw in this humble layman the heart of a man who was alive with love and power the way I had been as a teenager. I told him I had never heard anything like his reading of the Scriptures. I longed for it, coveted it, was jealous for it. But it reminded me of my long-gone past, and that made me ill.

Finally, one night in my hotel room in Selma, Alabama, Milt asked if he could pray for me. "Son," he said, "I sure do love you. You love Jesus, don't you?"

"I sure do."

And he started crying. "I feel so sorry for you, James. I've been hearing your preaching and following your ministry for six years now, and I've wept my eyes out. You're so tormented! I know you are chosen and anointed by God and you have a love for Jesus in your heart. But I've cast demons out of witches, drug addicts, Hell's Angels, murderers, and convicts, and I believe you are one of the most demon-assaulted men I've ever seen."

That shook me, because I hadn't thought demons could be a problem to a believer. Though I knew I was not totally free, I had not understood that I might be truly bound by the forces of darkness. Again, Milt asked if he could pray for me. I was tense and afraid. I didn't know if I wanted him to or not. You know, when you're in the presence of people who are clearly more spiritual than you are, who have the victory and are walking close to Christ, they make you nervous. It's as if their hearts and lives are huge beacons, showing you and everyone else the true limitations of your character. That was how I felt in front of Milt, especially in private. I could hardly pray anymore. What if he expected me to pray with him? Here I was, the big, hotshot, traveling evangelist, and my prayer life was zero.

But all Milt said was that he wanted to pray for me. How could I refuse? He asked me to sit in a chair in the center of my hotel room. Sprawled on the bed, I looked at that chair as if looking at the electric chair. A voice inside said, "If you get in that chair, you're going to die. It'll ruin your ministry and your reputation."

I felt strange sitting in the chair—like a little boy, totally humble before God and my new friend. If I could have prayed at that moment, I would have prayed that no one find out about what we were doing. Milt put his hands on my shoulders and quietly prayed from the Bible. As the words flowed, I realized that I didn't really know the Scriptures at all. Verses streamed from his lips like a living river, and tears streamed from my eyes. Milt knew the Word of God like I had never thought of knowing it. And all he prayed was the Word.

Then he shifted gears. He stepped out in the room away from me and addressed the powers of darkness with an authoritative tone. He told the devil to release me, in the name of Jesus. He stood against the powers of darkness in my life, calling on the name of the Lord Jesus to stop all the hordes of hell and every demon spirit that bombarded my heart and infested my life. I sat there, a man in chains. I was a child of God, but I was defeated, in despair. I was a man held captive by the enemy. If anyone ever needed to be restored, if anyone ever needed to be released, if anyone ever needed to be refreshed, I needed it.

He rebuked the devil and commanded him to depart. He bound evil spirits one by one and told demonic beings to leave me and leave the room. Jesus would have simply said that the man was standing there getting the weeds and briars out of my life, yet all I wanted was for him to finish quickly. It was humiliating. Fear dashed through my head. *What if someone hears him? What if one of my staff members overhears him talking to the devil in my room? What if my preacher friends find out about this?* I wished he wouldn't talk so loudly. I hoped the walls were well insulated. My reputation was uppermost in my mind.

When he was through, he sat on the edge of the bed and asked me if I felt anything.

"Milt," I said, "I didn't feel anything."

"You didn't feel like anything left you?"

I shook my head. "I wish I did, but nothing happened. I'm sorry."

Milt leaned toward me and spoke softly, a man standing on the Word of God, not living by sight but in faith. "*Son, it's all over.* That traffic against your mind, the power of the enemy against you, is broken in the name of the Lord Jesus through His blood and by His Word. James, you're going to start hearing God, and you're going to start seeing again what God is saying and doing." I smiled and shook my head, as if to say that that sounded wonderful but that I would believe it when I saw it.

Two days later I was back home when I was awakened early in the morning by tears rolling down my cheeks. Scripture flowed from my mouth as if I couldn't help reciting it. I quoted verses I knew I had never memorized, yet I knew it was Scripture. I shook Betty's shoulders. "Betty! Betty! It's gone, it's gone, it's gone!"

"What's gone, James?"

"Honey, the claw that was in my brain! It's gone! I can think! I can think! It's gone! It's gone!"

I grabbed my Bible, and the words came off the page like honey, like life itself, like fire. The Bible was alive in my hand and in my head and in my heart. I can go to the Word of God now and open it any place, and life comes off the pages. I do not go into the Bible to analyze, to get sermons, to just read. I go to it for nourishment and refreshment, for the very life of Christ.

God restored me. He freed me. I was truly delivered. But the battle still raged. I had to stand and resist the fiery darts of the enemy. I had to put on a shield of faith from then on. I had to walk in the Word, devour the Word, put it down inside me. I didn't just get some relief. I was freed. I was released to build walls against the devil in my life. I learned that if I didn't put Jesus and the Word first, I could fail again. I had to live by every word that came forth from the mouth of God, and in practical, how-to terms, that meant to immerse myself in the Bible.

People who want freedom and deliverance may get it and then lose it if they don't order their priorities and stay in the Word. Read it—daily. Pray constantly. Get back to Jesus and let Him fill your life so the devil can't invade the stronghold. You can go into the battle like a conqueror to scatter and defeat the enemy. You've been defeated; you felt like no one cared; you wanted not to live But there is victory in Jesus.

I was free! I was victorious! I loved Jesus again! I prayed, I read, I witnessed, and I blessed my wife and children. No one around me could have missed the dramatic change. My temper, my appetite, and my lust were under control. In a matter of weeks I lost twenty-two pounds. You couldn't *make* me fight. I was a new man, and all I wanted to do was to tell others about Jesus. I was busy about the Father's work, and I couldn't have been happier. And what about Betty? After having prayed for me for so long, she must have been thrilled to death, right?

Wrong. Let her tell it: "I'm sorry to say that I wasn't thrilled. I already had it in mind how God was going to make a change in our family. He was going to change James. I thought the problem was mainly his. I almost got mad at God. James was so caught up in the Lord, so in love with Jesus, it was as if I was losing my husband.

"I saw him ministering to others and giving his time to them, and I thought, *What about me?* I was full of self-pity, condemnation, doubt, and disbelief. I had worked so hard to be a good person, I didn't believe I was bad enough for Satan to really bother me. I thought, *Boy, James sure needs some help, but not me.* But I was deceived. I had as much or more work needed in my life than he did. The difference was, James had a teachable spirit. I didn't, but I didn't know it. I was just miserable.

"I decided to test James and to find out how real this was with him. I tried to pick a fight with him, but he was so sweet it was sickening. It made me so mad! He just loved me and loved me. If I wanted to argue, I had to argue with myself. I finally realized that it was truly the love of Jesus in him. I desired so much to please the Lord that I searched my own heart. I got into the Word and asked God to show me.

"One night when James was at a meeting on the other side of town and the children were in bed, I pleaded with God to speak to me and to show me where to begin. He's so gentle and so kind if we're willing to receive. He told me that one area in my life that had dominion over me was a spirit of fatigue. I worked very hard as a wife and mother, but even if I got eight or ten hours of sleep, by midmorning the next day, I was wiped out. Exhausted. No energy. When guests came over for the evening, it was all I could do to be kind. I wanted them to leave early so I could get to bed by eight. This went on for months.

"Rhonda came home from school one day and bent over my prone body on the couch. With tears rolling down her face, she said, 'Mama, I'm so tired of seeing you stretched out on that couch every day! What's wrong?' I couldn't tell her. I didn't know.

"The Lord told me that night that He was my strength, my source. He told me that there was a difference in being tired and being fatigued all the time. I confessed that I had surrendered to that fatigue, and He removed it from me.

"I also wanted so badly to do everything right that when someone told me that I had done something wrong, I was crushed. My pride would rise up, and I'd want to fight back because I felt as if I had disappointed someone. The answer to that dilemma came after I had suffered for several days with a pounding headache that immobilized me. It wasn't getting better, and I didn't know what was causing it. The whole family gathered around me and laid hands on me and prayed for me. Robin, who was about ten at the time, gave me a homemade card. The message was typical, but the P.S. read: 'Maybe God is trying to show you something.'

"That cut to my heart, but it was the truth. The children left the room, and I noticed that James had been very quiet. I said, 'Honey, do you see something? Is God showing you something I need to confess?'

"He said, 'Yes, I think he has shown me something,' and when he came to embrace me, I thought, *Uh-oh, it must be a biggie. I'm in trouble.*

"But I was hurting so bad, I said, 'Well, come on and tell me.'

"He said, 'I don't think you're going to like it.'

"I said, 'I don't care. Just tell me so I can confess it.'

"'Well, the Lord's showing me that you have an unteachable spirit.'

"'I do not!' Amazingly, I had energy to fight back even when I was hurting so badly. But James didn't argue with me. He just went on. I decided to pout a little, but the Lord wouldn't let me. He impressed upon me that I had asked Him to show me something. He had done it, and now He wanted me to confess it. When I did, the headache left me. This was the beginning of what would later be a wonderful and complete deliverance for me."

Betty's healing was only the beginning of several miraculous healings in our family, and I'm telling you, I became a believer in the supernatural healing power of God. Now I believe the Scriptures when they say that sin shall not reign, shall not have dominion in our mortal bodies.

Sitting under Jim Hylton, a preacher I had been warned to avoid, I heard him read Romans 8:11: "But if the Spirit of Him who raised Jesus from the dead dwells in you, He who raised Christ from the the dead will also give life to your mortal bodies through His Spirit who dwells in you." I sat in the front row of that meeting, and I didn't hear the speaker; I heard God. He came upon me and healed me right there. The various maladies that had for so long afflicted me were gone! My throat was clear; my head was clear; my allergies were gone; and so were my aches, my pains, and my fatigue. My prostate, my kidneys, and all my throbbing glands were healed. I was literally and spiritually a new man!

Betty was healed of all the doubts and fears she had grown up with. The Lord Jesus convinced her that He had brought us together to serve as one and that she was not to die a premature death. No one is better for me than she is. After so many years of feeling inadequate, she now knows that I consider her my number one, most important spiritual adviser. She interprets Scriptures for me in a way no one else ever has. She might not be able to do it in public, and she wouldn't want to be assigned to teach a class, but brother, she teaches me.

Rhonda, who had suffered from asthma all her life, was in the midst of one of her worst attacks and feared she might die when I prayed with her and commanded Satan and asthma to release her in the name of Jesus. It left instantly, and she hasn't suffered since then.

Randy had been to the doctor many times for serious gastritis, but one day he claimed victory over it in prayer and the Lord showed him through His Word that he could be free of the problem. He has had no more trouble with it.

Robin had one of the most dramatic healings. She had a large blister-type growth appear on her lip, and it kept growing for several weeks. It was painful and unsightly, though our Christian doctor said it wasn't cancerous. He recommended that we have it removed. We prayed about it and took her to a dermatologist who recommended a plastic surgeon because removing it would undoubtedly leave a scar.

It had been with Robin three months when Betty took her to the plastic surgeon. By now, it was the size of a marble and looked horrible. We were convinced he would remove it that day, but something came up and he was unable to. When they returned the next day, he scheduled the surgery for several weeks later. What a disappointment! It became difficult for Robin to eat or brush her teeth, and of course she was embarrassed by it.

Robin wasn't discouraged, though. She told Betty, "Mama, God told me He wants to remove it Himself." But when it became larger and more painful, we decided to call the plastic surgeon and insist that he move up the date of the surgery. He agreed to move it up a week. It would require Betty's returning early from a crusade, but we felt it was the right thing to do.

The Sunday night a week prior to the appointment, however, Betty went into intercessory prayer for Robin. The kids in her Christian school were praying for her, too, but Betty hurt so much for her that she said, "Lord, why can't I bear that burden for her?"

Betty says: "I went to bed that night weeping and praying for her. I dreamed that Robin put her hand up to her lip and that the growth fell off in her hand. When I awoke, I ran into her room, fully expecting it to be gone, but it wasn't. My heart was broken.

"I told her about my dream, and later that day she admitted that she was rehearsing her testimony for when God removed the sore. I pleaded with the Lord to honor her faith and not to

146

let her be disappointed. That night, Dudley Hall and his family prayed for Robin because they thought the sore looked more painful than ever. Before James left for a trip, we agreed in prayer that the thing would be gone by that Thursday.

"On Thursday, at four o'clock in the morning, Robin came running into my room and woke me up, so excited. 'Mother! Mother! Look! Look!'"

The Price

Just as in Betty's dream, the sore had fallen off in Robin's hand. They praised the Lord, and they wanted to call me, but they waited an hour so I could at least sleep till 5:00 A.M.

Betty has had two other healings of note. One was of a serious female disease called endometriosis. The other, though perhaps not as serious a problem, was more visible. She had suffered from deep warts on her toes for more than ten years. They went all the way to the bone, and twice she had them surgically removed. They were ugly, they were embarrassing, they were bothersome, and they could be painful. Finally, she asked the doctor to tell her all he could about the warts, what caused them and all the rest. When she came home, she told me, "Now I know exactly how to pray for this. All I'm asking you, James, is to agree with me."

I did, and as God is my witness, my wife's feet are now as soft and smooth as a baby's feet.

My daughter broke her toe, and I saw the fracture on the

x-ray. A toe can't be set, but she wanted to play soccer the next week, so we laid hands on it and prayed. It was healed, and she played. It was a miracle.

Probably the most important healing for Betty was in her mind. She recalls: "All my life I had a spirit of fear. Fear of rejection, fear of not pleasing enough. Even though James encouraged me and complimented me and built me up, I listened to Satan more. I thought a Christian just had to endure until Jesus came back. I learned that I can live and endure victoriously in Jesus."

She had another dramatic experience the following January when the Lord blessed our Bible conference in new and fresh ways. Many were saved; many lives were changed. We didn't get to our room until about 3:00 A.M. Saturday, and as we got into bed, Betty lay down with her back to me. She says she felt as if a bolt of lightning hit her, and she began to weep. "I couldn't control it," she says. "I wept and wept and wept. It was like nothing I'd ever experienced before."

I asked her, "Is God speaking to you?"

She nodded.

"Well, what's He saying?"

"James," she managed, "He's got His arms around me, and He's just loving me. He said, 'Peace, My child. I love you, and I'm pleased with you.' That was like music to my ears. It was just beautiful. I'd never heard Him say that directly to me before. He may have tried, but I didn't receive it."

Betty recalls: "He just kept loving me and loving me, and I just kept weeping and weeping. Finally, in my spirit, I said, 'Oh, God, stop. I can't stand it anymore.' His love is so great and powerful. From that night forward, the Lord expressed His love through me toward others. I was able to express myself in praise like I'd never been able to before. When the Spirit of God manifests itself in you, you can't keep it in. It's got to come out."

Well, it didn't take long for the word to get out about ol' James Robison. I'd been delivered. I was into the Holy Spirit. My wife was speaking in tongues. I had seen healings. People at my meetings were being healed and delivered. God had delivered me from denominational bondage and told me to share the message of personal restoration with all Christians. So, I began preaching to Pentecostals, Charismatics, mainliners, anyone who would listen.

But I have to tell you what happened to me within my own circles, within the Baptists—Southern, independent, and otherwise. The largest churches canceled me immediately, and many pastors wrote me unkind, sarcastic, stinging letters. All I was doing was obeying God, following His Word, and trying to help people get free from defeat and from the power of the enemy in tearing down the strongholds. It was no different from what had happened in the Old Testament when they had to drive out the enemy or the enemy took the land. I was trying to be as biblical as I could be, and my former colleagues got on me like they thought demons were only in foreign countries and there wasn't any evil spirit force in this country.

I lost 50 percent of my ministry's income. We had to immediately go off the air at thirty TV stations. Almost overnight, we fell $2 million behind. Some of the debts we incurred in 1981 we're still trying to crawl out from under. Many precious Christians were patient with us, some were excited, but we were devastated financially. Praise God, we never wavered, though, because we knew the new message was of God.

The peace of God ruled in my heart. I wasn't even angry. I just loved my enemies. I really did. They couldn't make me fight. Even though many of the leaders are still against me, the tide has turned with the people. Of the twelve thousand who attend my Bible conference, ten thousand are Baptists who want New Testament life in their churches.

The only Baptists who don't agree with where I am right now are not listening and haven't heard what I've been saying. The Baptist Christian, the Pentecostal Christian, the Methodist Christian, all true Christians know God and have enough understanding of His Word to know truth when they hear it and to recognize light when they see it. All they have to do is listen, and they'll know that this is truth that will set them free. If they keep their hearts open and their mouths shut long enough and don't watch the lights go off inside their spirits, they'll be thrilled.

This makes sense. It makes the Bible make more sense. It makes life make more sense. The more people hear it, the more they say, "Boy, all this fits."

I love my Baptist heritage. I love the Baptist family. I love the Baptist people. But I also love *all* God's people. I don't care who they are or what church they attend. I love them. We're God's people through Christ, not through some church or denomination or ritual or religion. God told me to take His message to everyone, including those in all the other circles. "Go and minister life to them," He told me. "They love Me. They're My people. Minister to anyone who has ears to hear."

Talk about getting crucified by religious groups. I mean, my own people, many of them, just cut me off. But friend, listen, when you decide to walk with God, Jesus says your enemies will be those of your own family. Don't get angry with them; don't be unforgiving. Go on with God—no matter what. I have joy unspeakable, full of glory and peace that passes all understanding. Where did I get it? I got it through Jesus. I'm right back there walking in the woods with Jesus where I belong.

I believe that everything God was through Jesus, He wants to be through the church. I believe He can, I believe He's able, and I believe He's eager to do it. Our availability and the timing of God is the key.

Faced with all the persecution, all I could do was to take comfort in Psalm 56 where the psalmist asks, "What can mere men do to me? All day long they've trampled on me. They've distorted my words. They seek to destroy me. But God is with me."

And then I read Jeremiah 20 where the prophet says, "Everybody goes out and maligns me with whispers, but God is with me like a champion." What a powerful message!

That's what God said to me when my former friends were jumping all over me. I was boycotted and blackballed, and people were afraid to come to my meetings. I've told some of my friends in the ministry that if they don't think intimidation is real and if they don't think peer pressure is real, they should put my picture in their bulletin and pretend that I'm coming to speak at their church in three weeks. They'll get threats and harassment they won't believe. It'll come by phone, by mail, and in person. My critics will tell them they're going to undermine their church, the membership will go charismatic, they'll go wacky, they'll bounce off the walls, they'll be slain in the Spirit, and they'll speak in tongues. The pastor will be told that his future is finished with the Southern Baptists.

I have been accused of everything, even of pulling people out of wheelchairs and dragging them. All I ever do is love people and pray over a crowd. I want to get the attention off me and onto Jesus and let Him do His work.

Worst of all, I was labeled cultic. That hit all the papers, and it hurt. Some people still think that the change in my life and ministry in 1981 was as drastic as if Jimmy Swaggart announced he had become a Catholic priest. They pervert what I'm saying. Nobody with true spiritual sensitivity can really listen and disagree with what God is doing. Not an individual on the face of the earth who knows anything about the Bible can sit and listen to the message and not go out and say, "That's true."

The attitude against me by my former friends and colleagues

must change. It is not healthy. And praise God, I'm seeing some signs of its thawing.

Through all the misunderstanding, turmoil and, yes, persecution, God had a purpose. He put me into a wider circle; I have made friends with people I might never have considered associating with before. I was the only preacher I knew of who was a personal friend of all the leading preachers on both ends of the spectrum: Billy Graham, W. A. Criswell, Charles Stanley, Jerry Falwell, Jim Bakker, Oral Roberts, Rex Humbard, Robert Schuller, Paul Crouch, James Kennedy, Tim LaHaye, and many, many more from the right to left and from the Fundamentalist to the Charismatic. All these men love Jesus. They all want to serve Him. They have different approaches, but they are brothers in Christ.

Many of them don't know one another. They might criticize one another without knowing where the other is really coming from. I have been able to encourage these men to get to know one another and to work together, to pray for one another. I believe God has specially equipped me as a go-between, a liaison, a facilitator of cooperation. I feel the burden to see the body of Christ pulled together. I know there will always be distinctions, but we agree upon so much. We *must* work together!

One reason is that God has also showed me that disease in our country is going to become more rampant than at any other time in our history. We're seeing it already with herpes and AIDS. The Lord showed me that the only cure for these diseases throughout the earth is going to be His power working through the church.

He told me that the natural processes of our bodies, if not interfered with or overcome by bad eating habits or by engaging in unnatural acts, will resist disease. No doctors, no matter how dedicated—and I thank God for them—would be effective against these diseases. I asked God very openly and directly why, if the church really walked in Spirit-filled power, we would need doctors. The Lord showed me that doctors are skilled, trained hands. We will always need them. God could heal a broken leg; He may heal it instantly, but it's not likely. A good, skilled hand would set it straight.

Jesus said to be a good Samaritan. What did the Samaritan do? He bound the man's wounds, put oil on him, and took him to where he could receive care. It can't be wrong to bind a wound, so there's no question that the skilled, trained hand of a physician is something to be appreciated.

God wants to heal disease. How do I know that? Because Jesus said He came to do the will of His Father who sent Him, and He healed. Jesus is the exact representation of God's nature (Heb. 1:3). Everything God is, Jesus is. Everything God does, Jesus did. We know it's God's will to heal, but we don't know why all the people aren't healed. We don't know why Jesus didn't heal all the people. We can't answer all questions, so I say, let's not argue about them. We shouldn't try to create a theology over something we don't know. When someone doesn't get healed, we just have to say, "We don't know why, unless God reveals it."

But God has revealed to me that diseases are going to become so rampant that unless the church moves in the power of the Holy Spirit and learns how to deal with them, there is no hope. The church has to learn. The power of God can heal AIDS. The power of God can heal anything. His power is the only thing that can. What a testimony the church could be if we could heal diseases that no one else could, through the power of Christ!

When I say that the Lord tells me things, people naturally want to know if I believe that I actually converse with God. Yes, I surely do. He does not speak to me audibly, but I seldom speak to Him audibly either. Some people are naturally dubious;

others think I've gone mad. Some say the revelation of the Scripture is all we need, but I tell them that they can't believe the Scripture and say that. Even pastors try to tell me that, but I ask them, "If the only way God talks is through Scripture, how do you know He called you to preach?"

Jesus and God talked together. As Jesus was in the world, so are we. If He communed with God, why can't we? Did He not say, "I'll send the Spirit, and He will guide you into all truth"?

Conversing with God is consistent with the Word and verifiable in the Word. Jesus said in John 10, "My sheep *know my voice*." The Lord spoke to Peter and even sent him an angel. John spoke with God and said he fell as dead before Him. Did they or did they not converse with God? Paul prayed that we would excel in the revelations of the Lord and in the Spirit. Any revelation God gives us will reveal Jesus. If it doesn't express Jesus' life, it's not good fruit: it's not of God. That's an easy test. God's communications with us will be consistent with His revealed Word.

Frankly, I think we all hear God, but we don't always discern His voice. We don't always know Who it is. We think maybe it's our conscience, and sometimes it is. We have thoughts that originate from ourselves, thoughts that originate from the enemy, and thoughts that originate from the Spirit of God. The key is discernment, which God will give to those who seek it.

I want to build my ministry on conversations with God. I don't want to do anything unless He tells me to do it. He has given me a vision for what He wants communicated to this generation, and I want to obey.

I found it very helpful when He showed me how to test love and know whether it's His love or fleshly love or Satan's love. He said, "My love is redemptive. Man's love is self-serving. Satan's 'love' is destructive." We have a lot of love in the church that wants to destroy a person because he's been wrong. In the flesh, we might want to use a person while claiming to love him. But God's love wants to redeem a person, no matter who or what he is or has done. That message became a sermon against judgmentalism and has touched many lives all over the world through my preaching.

Late last year, God told me that He wanted to "talk to My children like I did Jesus. And you must tell My people that they can fellowship with Me like Jesus did. They must get My Word out of that leather binder and get it into their hearts. That is My Word, but it is not Me. I want to talk to My people. Tell them they can fellowship with Me."

He cautioned me that if I told people this, "they're going to say you're not putting enough emphasis on the Bible. Emphasize that they can't even know My voice if they don't know My Word. Tell them. Go tell My people that I want to talk to them. And they can talk to Me."

One of the more recent messages God gave to me in conversation was that "*the* Word must became *a* word. *The* word is not *a* word, and you'll never know *a* word if you don't know *the* Word."

Believe me, that sounded as strange to me at first as I'm sure it does to you. Nothing in my mental processes allowed me to understand that concept on my own. I said, "Lord, explain that to me."

Conversing with God

God told me that the difference between *the* Word and *a* word is that *the* Word is the Bible, the revealed Word of God for the ages, and *a* word is that message He gives to His children for individual situations today. For instance, He gave Joshua *a* word about Jericho, and it became *the* Word for us because it's part of the Bible. But I could march around my hospital room—if I were sick—once a day for six days and then seven times on the seventh day, and I might not be healed. But if God gave me *a* word for my situation, if He told me what to do to show my faith or something to do to display obedience, I could follow that and be healed.

Last year I had a painfully wrenched knee that made it nearly impossible for me to walk. I waited for a word from the Lord on whether He was going to heal it or whether I should have surgery. Eventually, I felt led to have surgery. Had I had the surgery any earlier, I believe I would have shown a lack of faith. And those who are extreme on the healing doctrine may feel that by having surgery at all I caved in to self-doubt or a lack of faith. In my mind, it was a test. I proved God by waiting upon Him, and He eventually led me to surgery.

Did I prove that God doesn't heal today? Hardly! I was healed of all those mysterious maladies that had wracked my body for so many years. I felt as if I had picked up ten or twenty years of life overnight. So, I know God heals today. I've seen Him do it, to me, to every member of my family, and to many others in our conferences and crusade services.

God told me that one of the problems we modern Christians have is that we presume on His written Word. We see a promise or an action in the Bible, and we say, "There, I'll claim that. That's for me, too." He told me that the messages in His Word are, of course, true, but that not every word or action He gave or took with the saints of old can be applied to all of our situations today unless we receive direct communication.

Every word in the Bible is given for instruction or reproof, but my point is that God is still speaking today. He has a word for every dilemma you face, and it may be something more specific than you'll find in *the* Word but it's always consistent with the Scriptures. It's *a* word, and it's just for you.

We can read about Simon Peter walking on the water and say we believe it, we believe it. But then we can walk on the water, and we'll go straight to the bottom. Unless we hear Jesus say as He said to Peter, "Come to Me," we haven't the ability to exercise faith as Peter did. But when He says come, if we really believe, we can do it.

Then God showed me that His anointing was for everyone. I said, "You mean it's not just for special people you've privileged by setting apart?"

He said, "No, it is for everyone."

I said, "I don't understand." He answered me in the middle of the night when I turned on the bathroom light and it cast its rays

158

on my wife, asleep in bed. "See her there?" He asked. "Look at her. She's timid. She's not a preacher. Not a teacher. She's a housewife and mother. Look at her. She's anointed. She's anointed to be a wife and mother, and the same glory that is on you when you are in the pulpit is on her in this house. I'm on her just like I'm on you, and if anybody doubts it, all he has to do is to come into your home. He'll see the glory of God because My glory, My anointing, is on your wife. I have an anointing like that for everyone."

I couldn't wait to share that with her in the morning. It gave her great peace. She had for so long felt that she was not talented enough to be an evangelist's wife. She doesn't play the piano; she doesn't sing; she doesn't speak publicly. "I'm not great at anything," she would say. "I'm just a wife." But she's an anointed wife, and that makes her great. God revealed to us that anointing is a special touch for a specific task. Remember every article, even the unseen utensils, in the tabernacle was anointed with the same oil and power, even though they had different purposes.

It wasn't long after my personal deliverance, healing, and restoration that I realized I had some fences to mend. I knew so many great leaders, yet in my ignorance and denominational superiority, I had made fun of some of them. I had a great time poking fun at Oral Roberts and trying to make him look the fool. Many fellow Baptists had done the same thing.

When I asked for a time to meet with him, he graciously agreed to see me, not having any idea why a Southern Baptist preacher would want to talk to him. "Oral, I have sinned," I said. "I made fun of your nine hundred-foot Jesus and many other things about you, and I was just flat wrong. I shouldn't have done it, and I want you to forgive me."

He was so quick to forgive me that he made a joke of it. "Oh, that's all right," he said. "I didn't envision Him nearly big enough. He's a whole lot bigger than that."

People have asked me what I thought of Oral's dramatic vision. I don't have any problem with it. If he says he saw it, I believe him; if he didn't, that's his problem. When I was with him, he also told me of having seen an angel in his room. I've met a lot of people who have seen angels, and even though I've never seen one, I believe those people. A little handicapped girl on my program told of seeing an angel, and I want to tell you, it was a powerfully moving story.

I never set myself up to hear God. I don't go to a certain spot, put on special music, and look toward heaven. I simply try to stay in communion with Him in prayer, and sometimes He invades my thoughts. I was driving once, listening to some praise tapes, and it was as if the Lord blurted out a message to me. He spoke to my heart, "Steel sharpens steel."

I knew it was God, but I had no idea what He meant. "Steel sharpens steel," I repeated. "What does it mean?"

"That's why the church is dull."

I was still lost. "What do You mean, God?"

"It takes steel to sharpen steel, a diamond to cut a diamond. You can't cut steel with chalk, and you can't cut a diamond with glass."

I waited for more, but I heard nothing. "God, I'm sorry, but I still don't understand."

"Leaders are like steel," He explained. "Apostles, prophets, pastors, evangelists, teachers, they're like steel. The members of the church family are not steel, so they can't sharpen the leaders. My people gather around the brightness and the sharpness of the leader, but they're dull. So he becomes dull. It takes some other steel to sharpen that steel, another diamond to cut that diamond, to shape it, shine it, polish it. In order for a leader to be sharp, he's got to come together with another leader with the same anointing, the same temper or firmness. They have to come together with a common purpose because too often leaders come together only in confrontation. When you bring two sharp blades of steel together head on, they both become dull. But if they go at the same cause together—but from different angles—there will be friction."

"You want there to be friction, God?"

"Oh, yes! It's only you leaders who shy away from the friction. You pull back, but I like it. If you come together with friction, you both go away sharper, and then My people will be sharp."

The Lord led me to the Scriptures where I found that it takes an apostle and a prophet and an evangelist to sharpen a pastor, and it takes a pastor and a teacher to sharpen an evangelist. No church will ever be right until the leaders are honed by one another. Paul rebuked Peter. James, the pastor, corrected all the leaders. The apostles and prophets and evangelists learned from one another.

Today they don't. They use one another, accuse, criticize, and walk on one another. God told me, "My people need to come together. Oral Roberts will be missing something if he never comes together with Jerry Falwell. Jimmy Swaggart will be missing something if he never meets with Pat Robertson. James Robison misses something if he never spends time with Billy Graham. Satan doesn't want you to do this. He keeps you all too busy living in your own worlds."

I was with a leading Christian not long after that, and he made a disparaging remark about Jerry Falwell. He said, "Jerry ought not to be involved in politics. I don't think it's right."

I shook my head and said softly. "That's so unlike you."

"What do you mean, James?"

"You don't criticize people. You don't even know Jerry Falwell. You have no more place to say that he shouldn't be in politics than he has to say you shouldn't be doing what you're doing. As surely as God has called you to your area of ministry,

He has called Jerry Falwell to tell people to wake up and get out from under the pew. We're about to lose the country. That's a mission for him. It may not be your mission, but you need to bless him. Do you realize that he's a brilliant man, a loving man, and a very kind and gentle man? You need to get to know him."

My friend looked at me sheepishly and said, "You are so right, and I am so wrong. I'm sorry. I want to know him."

I said, "You need to." I was talking to Oral Roberts. He repented quickly—the mark of a great man.

When I shared the steel-sharpening-steel message with a member of my staff, he said, "That's biblical. Proverbs 27:17 says that iron sharpens iron and that by this shall one man sharpen another."

All I could say was "Praise God." I knew He would never contradict His own Word, but I had never read those verses before. He had spoken truth to me that was verified in His revealed Word.

I confess I absolutely marvel at the way God communicates to and through me. He and I actually talk with each other, just like you and I would if we were together. It isn't a matter of maybe it is or maybe it isn't. I'll stake my soul on it; I know it's genuine. I ask Him questions, and He answers me. It wouldn't be any more real to me if He wrote it on the wall.

I've always had a good Bible understanding, but when I was delivered and set free, I became so saturated with the Word that I can say, without boasting, that I know the Scriptures. Being full of the Scriptures, I know who's talking when I hear a voice in the spirit world. Some people hear voices and assume they're the voice of God when actually they're getting messages from the enemy. A grounding in the Word is necessary before boldly venturing into the spirit world. I do not believe God ever contradicts His word in Scripture, though He may say something that differs from our denominational interpretations.

In the spring of 1986, God told me clearly that the Scriptures were given so people would recognize His voice and that now He wanted to converse with them directly. I heard God say that, and I'm going to help people hear God. I'm already seeing businessmen and others—who were so entrenched in traditional religion that they can hardly believe their relationships with God now—who are having dreams and visions and conversations with God that have changed their lives. There's no doubt about it. If Peter ever had a vision, they're having visions.

Men in the Dallas area, some of whom are the most affluent in the city, are conversing with God in ways that would make any Christian's heart leap. That's exciting to me. That's life. That's what people want.

It even happens to me in the pulpit. About 90 percent of the time, I go into the pulpit with only a general idea of where I'm going. I'm most effective when my head is empty and my heart is full. God has told me that if I take care of my heart, He'll take care of my head. He'll tell me where He's going to take me and say, "Come along for the ride."

I like to hear God, and I'm able to hear Him and willing to hear Him through anybody. So when I listen to preachers, I'm not really hearing them. I'm listening for the Lord. The ones who seem to be hearing the freshest words from God always bless me the most.

In my listening so carefully to God, I was called into a new ministry. God gave me a new assignment. I can state it simply: to restore the church to New Testament life, to unite true believers, to make disciples of Jesus Christ who will do His ministry, to evangelize the whole world in the power of the Holy Spirit. I know this is a supernatural assignment, but I also praise God since He has provided the supernatural power and resources to perform it. I now preach in many unusual places and under unusual circumstances, but that doesn't mean I endorse a particular person's ministry. Who am I to endorse anyone, anyway? *Endorsing* is not one of my four *E*'s. Mine include *encouraging* believers, *edifying* the body of Christ, *exposing* the unfruitful works of darkness, and *exalting* the name of Jesus as Lord of lords and King of kings.

Because of my new calling of the Lord—to unite true believers—the James Robison Evangelistic Association is setting up programs to see that every viewing area in the country has access to our daily and weekly television programs. Normally, it takes a television station two or three years to become profitable for us, but we've added stations in major market areas and seen them pay for themselves within a month. We're growing at the rate of about ten thousand new supporters a month. We once hit a high of about 200 employees, but we have cut back to about 120 people and an annual budget of nearly $15 million. We're in a strong growth phase now, but we want to be stream-lined, efficient, and economical in these last days. We are also going to prepare primetime evangelistic TV specials for America and the entire world.

I firmly believe that the success of our ministry has been in direct proportion to our listening to God and to obeying His assignment, which I call simply a ministry of restoration. This restoring is not only corporate—from within the church—but also personal.

I want to deal with the personal aspect of restoration, for that should be one of the major ministries of this book to the lives and hearts of readers, but first I want to recount some of my involvement in the PTL and Oral Roberts controversies of 1987. Because of my unique calling to restore the church and the indi-vidual Christian to a first love of the Lord, I found myself in an unusual position when Jim Bakker was plunged into disrepute and Oral Roberts told of visions that brought him skepticism from inside the church as well as from the world.

A few years ago I might have pointed the finger at these men and called them down, one for his sin and the other for his extremism. But now here I am, called to restore, called to unify. I know that God does indeed speak to His servants in conversations, visions, and dreams, and all of a sudden I find myself on the side of love and forgiveness and reconciliation. Believe me, it would have been easier and seemingly more consistent with my history to have taken the traditional position—the one most other leaders took. That would have been easier on me and my family and my ministry and its finances, too. But when you've decided to follow God, you can't second-guess yourself. You have to do what is right *because* it's right.

For that reason I appeared on the Richard Roberts television program in February of 1987 and on PTL and Trinity Broadcasting network (TBN) in March. I believe God used what I had to say to bring some healing and restoration in both those situations.

A Word of Restoration to the Church

As I sat with Oral Roberts's son, Richard, on his TV show set, God gave me the essence of this message:

A theological debate has been raging as to whether God still speaks to men today. The media mock the idea that God has actually spoken to Oral Roberts. Can you imagine what the media would have done with the story of Abraham when God told him to sacrifice Isaac?

Regardless of how the natural man reacts, the fact is that God still does speak to men. God wants His people to learn another lesson from all this; He wants Christians to pray for one another in all circumstances. Even if they disagree or think others are wrong, they must pray for them.

God has shown me that if I stumble, the only people who will have a part in correcting me will be those who love me enough to pray for me, not those who criticize me. God has revealed to me that if we become judgmental of other Christians, even if they are wrong, we short-circuit all spiritual life and the ability to communicate with God. I cannot become another man's judge. I cannot become his critic. I must pray for my brother. I must lift him up.

When God sent me—a Baptist evangelist to meet with Oral Roberts—I came under divine order to ask his forgiveness. I did so because, as a Christian, a preacher, and an evangelist, I had criticized him. I had mocked and mimicked him. God convicted me. When I said, "Oral, I have sinned," God's presence invaded that room. It was as though the Lord was applauding, as though He was thrilled.

The Bible says that man hears God and *must* hear God. The disciples of Jesus heard God. Jesus said His sheep would know His voice. You, as a Christian, can hear God. You will get some signals the world will not understand, but you don't need a barrage of criticism from the Christian community. You need heaven flooded with the prayers of concerned, compassionate people.

Many people don't know it, but there is a revival at Oral Roberts University. My son has enrolled there because I told him, "I want you go where prejudice does not prevail, where the Holy Spirit at least has a chance to get in, and Oral Roberts doesn't preach a traditional, biased message. He hears what everyone says and loves everyone." The school is open to the moving of the Spirit of the living God. We must have that. God knows we've turned out enough traditional and prejudiced preachers; we don't need any more. The university is a potential instrument in the hand of God.

Later that month, I was in Washington, D.C., preparing for an excruciating schedule. I spoke at a pastors' luncheon and then at a crusade in Constitution Hall that same night. The next morning I went to PTL in Charlotte, North Carolina, where I ministered to their two thousand brokenhearted staff members.

Then before flying to the West Coast to appear on TBN with Paul and Jan Crouch, I addressed the nationwide PTL network audience:

"There is going to be no funeral here at PTL except the funeral of dead works and lifeless religion, and I would like to preach that service!

"God wants to lead us all to repentance so that He can restore all churches. He wants to pour His Spirit out on all flesh, and He will do so through people who will repent of their sins and their dead works and receive the fullness of God in the freedom of the Spirit and release the life of God to the ends of the earth.

"The stage is now set for that to happen, and it will happen in the spirit of prayer. God says we are to put on the whole armor of God, not to do battle with the church up the street or the preacher across town or the one on television, but to do battle with the powers of darkness that seek to deceive and destroy every church and every ministry. The Scripture also says that as we put on that armor of God, we are to do battle in prayer and supplication, praying always in the Spirit.

"When I repented several years ago of my tendency toward prejudice, I realized I had seen myself as a watchman. I had been critical of others. In truth, I had become more of a watch*dog* than a watch*man*. I wrote the book on growling at people. The watchdog threatens people. He will make you more conscious of him than the enemy you should be watching.

"I now contend that if you have a greater man-consciousness or self-consciousness or preacher-consciousness than you have a God-consciousness, it is impossible for you to worship in spirit and in truth. I had lashed out at everyone. I tended not only to *preach* judgment, but also to *pass* judgment.

"I believe that watchmen and preachers today want to help the body, but some have a tendency to think they have to get the tares out of the wheat field themselves. The Lord said that we are not to go into His field and rip out the tares because that hurts the little wheat. We preachers must expose the unfruitful works of darkness and the reality of the tares. We must expose enemy activity. But we cannot root the devil out. That is God's business.

"God showed me that I had encroached on His work, and when He changed my life, He set me free from that. It was a dramatic change. When you have a Baptist preacher who has been blessed by the Lord, and the Lord tells him the body is bigger than just the Baptist part, it takes a while for that message to get through. But God told me to take His message to the *whole* body. In order to do that, I had to accept the wrath of my own spiritual family. They were really unhappy when I started casting out demons. (I don't know why they wanted to keep them. They don't make good pets!) I got into a lot of trouble for casting them out and for praying for the sick. But God told me to do it, and I kept doing it.

"God told me that we must put down our idols. We must not idolize Jim Bakker, Jimmy Swaggart, a denomination, Billy Graham, or Jerry Falwell. All of us are mere men. There is not a lily white one in the bunch. Only Jesus is perfect. I believe all these men are pure in their hearts and want to please God, but that does not mean they are perfect in all their behavior. We must not expect them to be perfect. We must submit to God, refuse to criticize, and then we can build up the body of Christ.

"I will not slander my brother. I will expose unfruitful works wherever I see them and call to repentance any brother who may be caught up in them. That is not slander. That is restoration. But, remember, it is an unfruitful work when you make people more man-conscious than God-conscious. I want Christians to become so God-conscious that they can go to their churches and see Jesus—that they will feel that the only ones there are themselves and God.

"Jerry Falwell is getting the greatest heat right now from some who are saying, 'Why don't you just let that ministry go down? Can't you tell that God is trying to bring it down?'

"No, God is not trying to bring it down. He is purifying it, just as He is trying to purify the whole church, and any man who raises his hand to bring down that which God is seeking to exalt is letting himself in for trouble."

That evening I went on the Trinity Broadcasting Network television program with Paul and Jan Crouch, where I shared:

"Who would have thought that Jerry Falwell, Bailey Smith, James Watt, Richard Dortch, and possibly Tommy Barnett and Rex Humbard would all be in a room for a prayer meeting? That has happened, and man didn't do that. The players are in place, and they can present the most beautiful symphony if they will play in harmony. The only issue is who is going to direct the concert. I pray that all the players on the stage will submit to God the Father and allow Him to direct it. If they do, the world will see a symphony of praise and it will exalt Jesus unlike anything they've ever seen. . . .

"I preach judgment. I do not *pass* judgment. But that is not the way I was taught. Paul Crouch, I was taught to measure you as a Pentecostal. You were taught to measure me as a Baptist. I was taught that the things some people experience today are of the devil. I was taught that Jimmy Swaggart's music was barroom music. Now I know it's not; it's heavenly music.

"We were also taught to idolize men. Jimmy Swaggart is a great singer and he has a great message, but he doesn't have the *whole* message. He has just part of the message, and we are never to fix our eyes on just one man. God is showing us that. Men are fallen. Even the apostle Paul was not our example— Jesus is. He was redeemed and set apart and *became* holy in Jesus Christ.

"We are to preach and present a message of separation from

170

sin and sinfulness, but we must also understand that to refuse to forgive sin and to judge others is, in fact, sin. When we see someone who is wrong, we must correct and reprove, but we must do it with long-suffering and patience, and we must speak the truth in love. If people do not repent, we must also remember that it is God's business to deal with them as sons. He says He will correct them.

"Before I went to PTL, I was told that it was going to be painful and very costly for me. I said, 'Well, I'm following Someone Who paid a great price so James Robison could be forgiven, so Jim Bakker could be forgiven, so every sinner could be forgiven, and not only forgiven, but also restored.'

"A lot of people are dying out there in the pew, swallowing curtain rods to make themselves upright and choking to death on them. They are trying to look holy. I don't know what it is to *look* holy, but I've watched different ones telling people how to do it. I say you look holy by being like Jesus. He is holiness.

"I have found that Baptists—and we all know some who are really flowing in the Spirit—can be very unkind. I don't know if you know that or not, Paul, but I'm from a Baptist background, so I can talk about it. You probably used to say unflattering things about us in your Pentecostal churches, but I have to report that it was worse than you said it was. But I've found out about you Pentecostals, now that I've been going to your churches. You don't take a back seat to anybody when it comes to meanness. Did you know that? The ornery, mean stuff among some hard-line Pentecostals is enough to choke a goat, and it must be stopped. That is not the Holy Ghost. There's nothing holy about it. It's a spirit all right, but it's not a holy spirit. It's a religious spirit that causes people to be very, very unkind, and any spirit that causes you to treat other Christians with less dignity than Jesus showed Judas is not the Spirit of God. Jesus washed Judas's feet.

"It would settle a lot of the current mess if we could just get all the players in one room and wash one another's feet. I want a revival to come to the church in America that would bring about such cleansing, purification, and holiness that Jimmy Swaggart could hardly wait to get to PTL to preach a camp meeting! By the way, some people see Jimmy Swaggart as an enemy of PTL. I've heard the nonsense that he wants to take over that ministry. Jimmy Swaggart doesn't want anyone else's ministry. All he wants is the ministry of Jesus. I think he wants that for all of us. I believe he wants PTL to be pure. That's the only prayer he has for it. . . .

"Some of you are unhappy with me. You are saying, 'We don't need you.' You don't know how badly you need me. I *do* know how badly I need you. I refuse to be cut off from you. I'm not going to hide myself in some safe place and stay out of all the warfare. I'm getting right in the middle of it. I'm not afraid of the bullets. People are shooting at me from all sides because I choose not to join a camp.

"Only eternity will reveal how deeply I was hurt several years ago when God set me free from religious bondage. God had told me He had a message for the whole body, and it was to be preached, not to part of the body, not merely to the Baptist part, but to the whole. He said, 'James, you are to go without fear and preach to everyone, wherever I send you, and you are to do what Jesus did—all of it.'

"One thing in particular He said clearly to me: 'You are to pray for the sick.'

"I said, 'God, I've watched healers that are into extremes, and Lord, we Baptists don't believe in this healing. I just can't be something like I've seen in others, with all that phoniness.'

"The Lord said, 'I never told you to be like anyone but Jesus. My Son touched the sick. The disciples laid hands on them and anointed them with oil. I told the church to do it. I told you to pray for them whether or not they ever get well. Just obey Me. Don't do it because of the results. Do it because I said to do it, and I alone will give the results. I don't call you to perform. I call you to obey. I'll do the performing.'

"I said, 'Oh, God, it's going to ruin my reputation.'

"He said, 'But it's going to do a lot for Mine. You obey Me.'

"He told me to cast out demons. I went to church casting out demons and people cast me out. I didn't know people could be so fond of demons.

"You will never know the hurt it was to my heart that I was misrepresented. Only eternity can reveal how much I love the people who inflicted the hurt, every one of them. I never fought back, and I never will. I will never fight, even if they line up to kill me. Some are saying right now, 'We are going to destroy you, James Robison, for going to the aid of hurting people.' I may not have a ministry on television after April, but I don't worship my ministry. I don't have an idol. I will always have the ministry of Jesus, whether it's on television or not. It doesn't matter what people say. God has put a love in my heart for all my critics."

You Can Be Delivered and Restored

Much of the church has rejected the word of the Lord, and by that I mean the Spirit of the word and not the letter of it. The letter kills, but the Spirit gives life. When you reject God's Word, you are left with what kind of wisdom? Only the wisdom of the world—earthly, natural, and demonic (see Jas. 3:5), based on elementary principles of human society and religious traditions of men. So worldly principles teach conditional love—love based on performance. Worldly principles place burdens of law and works on people. Many are crushed under the load and others are puffed with pride or whitewashed with hypocrisy. They have trusted in external displays of power, and they have sought counsel from men and not from God, all to their ruin.

The ministry of the "Good News" is being taken away from some of the highly visible ones, who seemed to have it all together and is being given to others. Many in positions of leadership in the church have let greed and lust for power corrupt their callings. They have resorted to deceit to exploit people and build private empires. They have ministered to hurting people too often with mere words. Little has been done to minister the real peace that comes with the sure knowledge that Christ is your life, and that in Him you have a pure heart before your loving Heavenly Father.

God always goes to His people with love and forgiveness when they get on the wrong track. His mercy endures forever— it is always available. But that forgiveness and mercy is of no value to those who refuse to see the pain their conduct is causing and refuse to acknowledge that they have been wrong and stand in need of God's restoration. They fall, not because God wants them crushed, but because they reject His loving alternative.

God reserves vengeance for Himself, and with good reason. Men tend to misdirect vengeance. More often than not they take it out on their brothers, instead of on the real enemy, Satan. God is purifying His church. He does not need a corps of hit-men to do His work. If you hear a message that obviously does not have the purpose of redeeming and restoring people to a right relationship with God, though it may be labeled "love" or "truth," that message is not of God. If someone is exposing a fellow believer in a destructive way, he is not "clothing the naked." He is pointing the finger and God forbids that (Isa. 58:7,9).

In the interest of religion and idolatry, some try to destroy others. In so doing, they put themselves in the place of God. That's a dangerous place to be. Jesus Himself said that He did not come to judge man (John 3:17) and that not even the Father judges but has committed all judgment to the Son (John 5:22).

Today is the day of our opportunity to lift up the real Jesus that He might draw all men to Him (John 12:32). And how do we lift Him up? By doing the works that He did, which as you'll remember were works of love (John 13:34).

Hebrews 3:1 says we have been made to share Christ's heav-

175

enly calling. Jesus spelled out that calling in Luke 4:18–19. It is to 1) preach the gospel to the poor; 2) proclaim release to the captives; 3) give sight to the blind; 4) free those who are downtrodden; and 5) proclaim the favorable year of the Lord—that is, this time in which God imparts righteousness simply on the basis of faith.

Nothing in that calling instructs believers to point out one another's faults or hold their brothers or sisters up for public ridicule. Faults must be dealt with, but that is not the way. God tells us in many passages how we can relate to one another constructively and redemptively. Galatians 6:1–4 presents the Spirit of God's Word with exceptional beauty and clarity: "Brethren, if a man is overtaken in any trespass, you who are spiritual restore such a one in a spirit of gentleness, considering yourself lest you also be tempted. Bear one another's burdens, and so fulfill the law of Christ. For if anyone thinks himself to be something, when he is nothing, he deceives himself. But let each one examine his own work, and then he will have rejoicing in himself alone, and not in another."

First, our motive in dealing with the fault must be to restore, not to destroy.

Second, our purpose in ministering to the brother at fault is to *bear* his burden, not to *bare* it. We are to take the load of sin and guilt off him, not to heap more on him.

Third, we are to realize that this is how the law of Christ is fulfilled. The law of Christ is the law of love, not of condemnation.

Finally, we must keep in mind that we are all saved by grace, not by our works or because of our merit. We must remember that the law of sin indwells all of us (Rom. 7:23).

And that leads me to a personal word of healing and restoration for you, brother or sister. This is the foundation for the messages I preach six days a week on television from our studios, and we tape everything I do on the road in conferences and seminars and citywide crusades. My teaching, and that of my many associates, is also based on the fundamental message of personal restoration, such as I received from the Lord several years ago.

Ephesians 2:19–22 says, "Now, therefore, you are no longer strangers and foreigners, but fellow citizens with the saints and members of the household of God, having been built on the foundation of the apostles and prophets, Jesus Christ Himself being the chief cornerstone, in whom the whole building, being joined together, grows into a holy temple for the Lord, in whom you also are being built together for a habitation of God in the Spirit."

We're being built into a holy habitation, literally a holy of holies, a dwelling place of the Lord. We're being built! This is happening. This is progressive action. This is New Testament. The glory dwelt on Jesus and now He wants that glory to dwell on the church that's being built. When Christ comes, He's coming for a people adorned in His glory—holy, blameless, spotless, washed in the Word, sanctified in truth.

My calling in this age of despair is threefold, as God has revealed it to me. I am to preach the message of Christ, do the ministry of Christ, and fulfill the mission of Christ. His message is repentance. His ministry is the example He set and modeled for the world. And His mission is redemption, world evangelism.

Fulfilling this three-fold calling impels me to be open to the work of God in the lives of other individuals as well as to His work through other ministries and faith groups. For the Church as a whole to function in health and strength, all of its members must be well and free to do their part. Consequently, all spiritual gifts must be recognized, received, and encouraged. The supernatural power of the Holy Spirit must be acknowledged and released by the Church as expected and commonplace, not as something weird and frightening.

From the time I was called to preach, I have believed that all the gifts existed for today, but God has grown in me an understanding of the gifts and how they are to be used. He began teaching me about them when I was only nineteen and discovered two knots, larger than silver dollars, in my chest. They had become so painful that it was difficult for me to button my shirt. If anyone even brushed up against me and touched one of those knots, I would have screamed.

During a revival meeting, I told the crowd that I was going to have surgery the next week and asked everyone to pray for me about the sore spots. After the service, a Pentecostal man sought me out and asked if he could pray for me. (That was before I had been taught that Baptists were not to let Pentecostals pray for them!) I was just a simple disciple of Jesus, so I let him. We went into the pastor's study, just the man and I. I began to tremble. The man laid his hands on me with a gentle touch and rebuked the tumors, then began to speak in tongues. It was beautiful. My spirit bore witness with his spirit, though I did not understand his language. The next morning when I got up, the knots were gone. I never had that surgery. The removal had been performed painlessly by the Great Physician.

Because many in the Church today do not understand these manifestations, having relegated the power of God to a past era, they have criticized me and warned others against my ministry. In fact, for a brief period, unbelief interrupted the great flow of God's healing power in my life. People who didn't understand what had happened to me began to criticize and ridicule me. Their remarks appeared in the public media.

I returned to an annual convention of pastors and church leaders at which I had been welcomed and greeted as a friend a year earlier. Now these same people avoided me. As I walked among them, they turned their backs on me. In their private conversations, they condemned me and made false and malicious statements about me.

I allowed this faithless and unloving behavior to wound me so severely that the Holy Spirit's ability to move through me freely was quenched. Some of my prayers for the sick were ineffective. Yet another work of restoration had to take place within me. I had to acknowledge God's love for me in order to restore my broken spirit and receive His grace. That enabled me to respond with love and forgiveness to these Satan-inspired attacks. I am not angry with these brothers and sisters as I would have been before my restoration by the Lord. I know what they are thinking and feeling because, to a large degree, I have been there myself. God has made it possible for me to love them and pray for them. Free from bitterness, once again I could move in healing power.

Through one other difficult personal incident, God showed me how Satan can use pride to stifle healing and keep God's people in bondage to illness. After the Lord had moved through my body with His wonderful healing power, the allergic reactions, sinus headaches, throat infections, and every uncomfortable and disabling symptom left me. I never felt a twinge of any of them until one day I sensed the making of a sinus or a tension headache. The pain hit me like two darts, one in the back of the neck and the other protruding upward, through my sinuses. I sensed Satan had sent these two arrows to pierce me, and I immediately searched my heart to see if I was living in rebellion against God at any point. I thought He might be trying to get my attention by allowing the enemy to attack.

The Spirit did not seem to be convicting me, so I said to the wicked one who had sent the arrows, "Go away!" The pain didn't go way; in fact, it intensified. A young staff member was sitting in my office, and the Lord told me, "Tell him you have a problem; tell him you're getting sick, that you feel a headache coming on. Get up and walk around your desk and kneel and tell him you want him to pray for you."

In the past, I might have resisted such a humbling display. This man was younger, and he was a subordinate. But I answered silently, "Yes, Lord, I will do that. I'll kneel and ask him to pray for me."

The moment I expressed that to the Lord, the darts left my neck and head. Immediately, I understood what had happened. Satan doesn't want to be exposed. He doesn't want people humbling themselves before one another. He doesn't want them uniting in prayer against him and bearing one another's burdens. He was glad to inflict pain upon me, but when he realized how I was going to deal with it, he left.

I refused to let him get away with that. Smiling at the puzzled staff member, I told him about the pain and that I had intended to humble myself and ask him to pray for me. "We're getting the devil coming and going, " I said. "I'm not only free from this attack, but I'm exposing the devil anyway. You are learning while he's getting kicked in the teeth."

God wants you restored. He wants you free. The devil may say to you that you have to get to me, James Robison, to get help. Or you're going to have to get to some other preacher or healer or leader. That's a lie. Deliverance by man is vain. God alone will set you free. I do believe it's important that when you've been living in defeat, you confess your sin to another person, as the Bible says. There's something about confessing a need, confessing where your heart is, that is therapeutic and helpful. You won't regret it.

You don't have to go into all the specific, gory details. There's no need to take the past like garbage and lay it out on the table for everyone to see. But if at this moment you're living in defeat, you need to ask God for deliverance and get someone else to agree with you in prayer. It can be anyone of like faith. It doesn't have to be some great Christian. Just find someone who'll believe God with you.

You don't simply want relief. You want release from the power of the enemy. If you know those spirits that have come against you—spirits of deception, defeat, rebellion, rejection, intimidation, suicide, depression, lust, immorality, sensuality, perverseness, anger, murder, mockery, skepticism—don't be ashamed to admit that you've been deceived or defeated by a spirit.

This very day can be the day of deliverance for you. I went from the top of religious success to the pits of despair, to the point of depression and near suicide. I was not only deceived and defeated, but I was also diseased and nearly destroyed. I've been where you are. I've been at the bottom. I know what it is to fail, and I've hated myself for my failures. But God gave me the grace to forgive myself and the grace to forgive others. He healed me, restored me.

The good news is, it can happen to you. You can be restored to health. You can be set free. Don't put it off. Get help. You don't have to live in defeat. You can live as an overcomer. In the midst of the battle, you can be more than a conqueror.

You need to forgive everyone you've been angry with or bitter toward. And then you need to forgive yourself, knowing that God Himself forgives you. Then, when you've found someone to pray with you and stand against the devil, commanding his demons to leave you alone in the name of Jesus Christ, you will be restored and delivered. Then stand on guard against further attack. Immerse yourself in Scripture and fellowship with other believers. And get to work in the kingdom. There's a great and mighty work that must be done. You can become part of the restoration of the Church as a whole. Turn your eyes outward; quit focusing on yourself.

Then, out of the abundance of your heart, let your mouth confess what God has done for you. Tell someone! You have personal restoration in Jesus. You have release. You have forgiveness. Your friends and neighbors are longing for this blessing. Your witness may allow then to experience the abundance of God's love.

Share Jesus' calling with me. Proclaim release. Give sight to the blind. Free those who are downtrodden. And proclaim the twenty-first century as the favorable year of our Lord!

You Can Be Called to a Special Work

If you are just an ordinary believer, you have as much healing power in you as Oral Roberts or James Robison. The day is approaching when belief in healing will be so strong and there will be so many dedicated and true disciples that each sick person will have their choice of healers to lay hands on them, anoint them with oil, and pray over them.

At one of my meetings I saw a woman in a wheelchair who had been in pain and unable to walk for years. After I had preached, a layman laid hands on her and prayed a prayer of faith. She was completely healed. In another meeting, a blind, deaf, and mute girl received complete healing, not in response to my prayer or that of any other person in the limelight, but as the result of the prayers of ordinary believers.

As the restored Church of Jesus Christ unfolds, Satan won't be able to continually defeat even the least of its disciples. Children will lay hands on the sick and pray for them, and they will be healed. Teenagers will cast out demons and deliver people from bondage. Miraculous healing will take place in the body of Christ not because home Bible studies have been stamped out but rather because they have sprung up everywhere. They will release the power of God throughout the land.

Believers will drive across the country, praying for the sick, raising the lame from their beds and putting Satan to flight at every turn. This will be the pattern, not only in the big churches, but everywhere the Church gathers as God-fearing believers. The miracles will be of such an extraordinary nature that it will be impossible to credit them to anyone but Jesus. It will be obvious to all that they are seeing His Body functioning as it was designed to, because it will have been healed and restored to perfect health.

We are already seeing glimpses of these miracles where God's people seek Him and allow Him to give them unity in the bond of peace. I am seeing hundreds upon hundreds of such miraculous manifestations.

One of the greatest examples of what can happen to those who are willing to let God change their minds is found in the story of Terry and Susan Moore of North Dallas, Texas. They were born-again Christians, members of a local fundamental Bible church. He was an oil company executive with a violent temper, usually directed toward inanimate objects that didn't work; she was a shy housewife, articulate in private conversations, petrified of public speaking.

They had, for several years, regularly attended the meetings of the James Robison Evangelistic Association's Inner-Circle. These were small Bible conferences in hotels in various cities where we invited two to three hundred of our most faithful giving and praying partners. The purpose was to show our appreciation for them and to minister to them by allowing them to worship and study under various preachers and teachers and to fellowship with others they had met at similar gatherings.

Many of our Inner-Circle friends made it to several such conferences and developed lifelong friendships. When the Moores attended our meeting in August of 1982 in San Antonio, they had been to enough of these meetings that they traveled there with five other couples. The conference began Thursday evening and ended Sunday noon. That was a monumental conference, because for the first time, I would be sharing what had happened to me. Many of these friends were Southern Baptists, independent Baptists, Bible churchers, and the like. As with me, their first exposure to a more dynamic, more alive and active faith—I knew—could cause consternation. I didn't know if I would lose these supporters and friends, or whether they would see what I had seen, experience what I had experienced.

The Moores, whom I knew personally, had heard that something had happened to me. They were curious, excited, eager to know more. When I began the Friday session with, "I want to share what's changed my life," Terry leaned over and whispered to Susan. "That's what they always say." He wasn't putting me down. He had grown up a Baptist, and he had heard that phrase in testimonies and sermons all his life.

They were surprised when I did not preach. I did not teach. I did not share my personal story of restoration. I read from the Bible. That's all. I simply read. If lives were going to be changed, it would have to be by the Word of God alone. Susan Moore remembers, "It was not man's word. It was God's Word and we finally heard it, saw it. Our eyes were opened. We took the Word literally."

On Saturday, just before we broke for lunch, I mentioned to the crowd that if anyone was interested in praying for deliverance, we would reconvene at one o'clock. Our normal practice at these gatherings is to leave the afternoons free, but this optional invitation was given to all. I was stunned when everyone returned, even those few couples who had been upset at the di-

185

rection they sensed I was going from what I had read—about the gifts, healing, prophecy, deliverance.

At that afternoon session, I spoke briefly about my own deliverance and then asked if anyone wished to come forward so that we could pray with them to be set free of bondage in their lives. People didn't wait for others to get out of their way. They moved chairs, sometimes even tipping them over, to get to the front. It was like opening the doors of a cattle truck after an eight-hour drive. The Moores were there, too.

Terry was delivered from a spirit of anger that had caused him to ruin more than one tool or piece of sports equipment. He had a short fuse and if something failed him, he bashed it and then trashed it. Susan was delivered of a spirit of fear that had made it impossible for her even to share her testimony, unless she was just talking privately with a friend. "If I had to speak in front of a group," she recalls, "It was as if my breath caught in my throat."

Most important, the Moores' minds and hearts were opened to put behind them denominational superiority and tradition, to take God literally, to believe that the gifts of the Spirit are for today. "We believed in them, practiced them, desired them, wanted them. We wanted anything Jesus had in store for us."

One of the couples that had traveled with the Moores to San Antonio started out very skeptical about what I was espousing, but they were guests and couldn't leave. By the end of the conference, they had been won over. On the way home from the airport in Dallas, the couples asked each other, "What happened to us?" They all knew their lives had been changed, but they didn't know what would come of it.

The Moores found that when they got home, they had an insatiable desire for the Word of God. "We wanted the Lord," Susan says. "Terry sat out on our back porch during every spare minute for a year, poring over the Word, studying, reading, quoting, memorizing. We were hungry. God had put a hunger deep within our hearts to study, and now He was filling us up."

Because the Moores' church had no Wednesday night services, they were not in conflict when they began praise services at their home. It started with just them and another couple, praying, singing a cappella, reading Scripture. Sometimes, the entire evening's exercise was the four adults, taking turns reading chapters from the Bible.

When they invited anyone who wanted to come, they didn't know how many would show up. Sometimes it was just the four of them, sometimes eight, sometimes twenty-five. Some of their closest, most intimate friends from their church joined the Wednesday night fellowships. The meeting was open to anyone who wanted to praise and worship the Lord. The Moores remember that at first they were acceptable to their pastor and other people at their church, because they had not been led into all the manifestations of the gifts. "We were normal. Not radical."

But once they began to prophesy, to dance in the spirit, to see deliverances and healings, the time came when they knew they had to separate from their church. "We didn't leave as inconspicuously as we should have, as we would today," Susan recalls. "About six months later, Terry felt led to go and ask the pastor's forgiveness for the strife."

They left their church in June, and by September of 1983, they prayed and gave their ministry to God. They pledged to remain faithful and committed no matter how many people showed up. As soon as they had surrendered that to the Lord, the attendance increased. Their little Wednesday night fellowship has grown to become the Sojourn Church of more than two hundred members. Terry is the pastor, and the church is not bound by tradition. "We speak in tongues, prophesy, deliver, heal, dance unto the Lord, sing, raise hands, whatever," Susan says. "But it's all rooted in Scripture."

They are on such good terms with their former church that Terry has teased the new leadership that they should, "Send any of your strange ones to us, and we'll send our normal ones your way."

"God did it," Susan concludes. "We were just in the stream. We didn't plan any of it. We're not crusaders. This kind of exciting, dynamic, Spirit-filled life is available to anyone who is willing to go with God, to lay down their ideas of who God is and let the Word speak for itself.

"There is freedom in Jesus. It's so good to be free. Jesus is so alive, so real. We just pray that people will see Jesus in our meetings because of our love for one another. People want to see a living God. It's so exciting to see healing and deliverance."

Susan says Terry prayed for a man to be delivered who seemed to inflate to twice his size, turn red, and fall to the floor when Terry commanded the enemy to be gone. The man was delivered from a spirit of rejection that had plagued him all his life.

The Moores counsel believers who come to this new knowledge of the possibilities in Christ to change churches, if the Lord leads them, but not to get out from under the authority of their pastor, even if he's wrong. He's been put in charge over you, and until the Lord leads you elsewhere, he's your spiritual authority and protection, even if you disagree with him.

The bottom line is that the Moores were lay people from a traditional church. They wound up doing the work of Christ themselves, not waiting for a James Robison or some other leader to do it. They ministered to others and others ministered to them. You see, the day of the superstar is over in the Church. The day has come when all will do the ministry of Jesus. Some people may become as involved as the Moores; others may wish to be part-time volunteers for Jesus.

In the Restoration, believers will have to learn to focus on Jesus, not on men. They may stumble and make mistakes, but

Christians won't be butchering and ostracizing each other. When some do slip, they will be restored in a spirit of love.

Christians can't imagine what God plans to accomplish through the healthy Body He is preparing, but He must first get us to be still and know Him. He must have us holy, showing us the error of what we have been taught: that it's normal to live in defeat, that's it's not not normal to overcome.

To become overcomers, we must get practical, and this is where the rubber meets the road. God must have our attention and our time. Believers must be willing to make a commitment to spend time with God, presenting their minds to Him. He promises to renew our minds (Rom. 12:2).

Appallingly, some of the Church's leaders seem to be the worst obstacles to serious Bible study. A pastor of a large church expressed his dismay over a proliferation of home Bible studies among his congregation. "These things are always getting out of control," he told me. "People get drawn into all kinds of error."

He was typical of many mainline, established preachers. In their insecurity, they are afraid to see their congregations begin to seek God, to delve into His Word, to hear Him and get excited about what God is doing. They view this as a threat.

To some degree, I have been guilty of the same insecurity syndrome in the past. Almost all of us ordained and established preachers have trained people, not to hear God but to assemble themselves together and listen to us. This is not the way it was in the early Church. There were no big buildings or coliseums for large group gatherings. The church met in homes where people had the Bread of Life broken to them in small groups. Far from being fragmented and destroyed, the Church grew and became powerful enough to turn its world upside down.

I constantly emphasize the necessity of hearing God through a diligent involvement in His Word (Ps. 119:11). Ever since I answered God's call to preach the gospel, I have been hearing preachers' and sincere believers' yearning and praying for genuine revival. That revival will come when believers, as humble individuals, experience true revival in their hearts. And that will happen when they so desire to see His glory and to dwell in the land that they seek His Word above all else. To be true disciples and overcomers, believers must know who they are in Christ, and they can, only through the Word of God.

A word of caution: I am delighted at the new freedom believers feel in their expressions of praise and worship. If people filled with the Spirit feel like lifting their hands or making utterances or even moving their feet in a reverential dancing motion, I believe they should be free to do so. But I believe with equal conviction that anyone who does not desire to lift his hands, make utterances, or dance should be free not to.

Unfortunately, I have seen people try to force others to speak in tongues or be slain in the spirit or do some other things for the sake of performance or conformity. I have watched in spiritual agony as people have been manipulated and intimidated into coming forward to get the Holy Ghost or get anointed with oil or get baptized in the Spirit or get the gift of tongues.

The Scriptures and experience has shown me that God brings people along at their own paces. He gives different ones different gifts at different times. Actually, every Spirit-filled person has all the gifts, though God chooses to use certain gifts more than others with certain people. I have had some tell me they spoke in tongues, but only once or perhaps two or three times. Each time, God had a work or a purpose to accomplish in their use of the gift. The Scripture clearly teaches that tongues will edify the individual believer and can be developed. I have also known people whose lives are so anointed, so obviously controlled and empowered by the Spirit, that only a sceptic or deeply prejudiced person would doubt they are Spirit-filled, and yet they have never spoken in tongues.

I believe every Spirit-filled believer can pray in tongues. It is sad that Satan has made it such a divisive issue. Some idolize the gift while others criticize. Paul clearly said "forbid not to speak in tongues" (1 Cor. 14:39). The Spirit activates different gifts in different people as the needs arise in the Body. The choice is based on the believer's availability, not his ability, and is made at the discretion of the Spirit. We may never know why He gives a certain gift to one believer at one time and a different gift to another believer until we are called home to Him. But we *can* see and know the work done through those gifts to bless the Body of Christ and glorify His name.

God is saying to the whole Church, "Come and receive what I have for you; I am calling you for a special work, and I want to equip you for that task." It has been thrilling to see the genuine gifts exercised effectively and beautifully to minister to the Body and to bring glory to God. It's exciting to watch born-again, Spirit-filled Methodists, Catholics, Pentecostals, Baptists, Episcopalians, Charismatics, and Fundamentalists praying for someone and then hear some of them speak in tongues while others pray in English. Then, to see the afflicted one miraculously healed, not because of the utterances but because of the love and faith they all shared in their hearts.

Jesus did what He saw the Father do (John 5:19). He said His disciples were to do what He did (John 14:12). We are to follow His example. Did He rebuke His disciples for using their spiritual gifts? No! He rebuked them for *not* using their gifts, for desiring to misuse their power, and for suggesting that others be forbidden from using theirs. We must not criticize and rebuke those who exercise their gifts. We must follow Christ's example.

When that which is perfect comes, Paul said the partial will be taken away (1 Corinthians 13:8,9). Tongues will cease. Words of knowledge will pass away. But so will prophecy, witnessing, proclaiming the Gospel to the unsaved, and everything else we have known as important elements of the Christian life. Those things will no longer be needed. The race will have been run. All whose names have been written n the Lamb's Book of Life will be residing at their new addresses in the heavenly places. All that will be needed then, and all that will remain, are the big three—faith, hope, and love.

And the greatest of these, both on earth and in heaven, is love. Love is the pattern Jesus calls us to follow, and in His work of restoration, God is going to erase every pattern but that. Then, in love, all the gifts of the Spirit will be exercised until the Bridegroom comes to receive His spotless Bride.